RISKY TIMES

How to be AIDS-Smart and Stay Healthy

A Guide for Teenagers
by Jeanne Blake

Introduction by Jerome Groopman, M.D.

WORKMAN PUBLISHING, NEW YORK

Library of Congress Cataloging-in-Publication Data
Blake, Jeanne, 1952-
Risky times: how to be AIDS-Smart & stay healthy: a guide for
teenagers/by Jeanne Blake: introduction by Jerome Groopman.
p. cm.

Summary: Explores the issue of AIDS, discussing such aspects as
sex, condom use, peer pressure, drug use, and decision making.

ISBN 0-89480-656-4

1. AIDS (Disease) – Prevention. 2. Teenagers – Health and
hygiene. [1. AIDS (Disease)] I. Title.

RC607.A26B59 1990 616.97 9205 – dc20 89-40728-CIP AC

"How Would You Feel?" exercise on pp. 132-133 is reprinted by permission of the National Institute on Drug Abuse, Washington,
D.C., from AIDS AND THE IV DRUG USER: A Training Program in Education, Risk Assessment and Treatment Planning for
Drug Abuse Program Counselors. Copyright © 1987.

Book and cover design: Charles Kreloff
Cover photograph: Walt Chrynwski
Photography sources: See page 155.

Workman Publishing Company, Inc.
708 Broadway
New York, N.Y. 10003

Manufactured in the United States of America
First Printing May 1990
10 9 8 7 6 5 4 3

DEDICATION

This book is dedicated to the many people with AIDS who have enriched my life.

CONTENTS

Bo Jackson

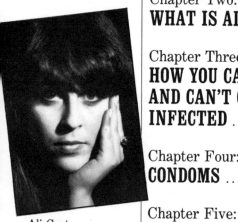

Ali Gertz

The AIDS quilt,
Washington, D.C.

Cher

AUTHOR'S NOTE

As a television news medical reporter, I am often invited to speak to groups of young people at schools, churches, and synagogues. The questions I am asked most often are about AIDS. What are the symptoms of AIDS? How do I know if I have it? Can I get AIDS from kissing? When will there be a cure?

These are good questions that deserve thorough answers. I have learned about AIDS from some of the finest teachers in the world—leading AIDS researchers and courageous men and women living with AIDS. I wrote this book to share what I have learned. I hope that as a result, fewer people will become infected with the AIDS virus and that people will be more understanding toward those already infected.

—Jeanne Blake

INTRODUCTION

In the decade I have cared for people with AIDS, I have found most striking, most devastating, that AIDS is largely a disease of the young. Suffering and death are not events we usually associate with the teenage and young adult years. But this disease has entered our lives and dramatically altered our patterns of behavior—not necessarily for moral reasons, but because it is a fatal disease.

Infection with the AIDS virus cannot be removed from one's body. Although drugs have been developed to slow the deterioration of the immune system, there is no cure.

But in most cases, AIDS can be avoided, and education is the best way to do that. By accepting our vulnerability, and by understanding the facts about AIDS, we take the first steps toward preventing it. We therefore must enlighten ourselves, confront issues that may make us uncomfortable, arm ourselves with information as a defense against the virus.

Risky Times, by providing clear, straightforward, scientifically accurate information about this deadly disease, will make an important contribution in the decades to come. Every case of AIDS is a tragedy and a loss, and it is folly to ignore the fact that young men and young women are at risk. Teenagers, don't function with a false sense that only "other" young people become infected—protect yourselves by learning about AIDS.

The intellectual and emotional understanding of author Jeanne Blake, her longtime involvement in the medical and social issues of AIDS, and her particular sensitivity to and understanding of teenagers have equipped her well to write this unusual book. *Risky Times* should be read by every young person and should be available in every home, classroom, library, church, and synagogue. It is a book that can create awareness and understanding—a book that can save your life.

—Jerome E. Groopman, M.D.
New England Deaconess Hospital
Harvard Medical School
Boston, Massachusetts
February 1990

Left to right:
Alexei, Ben, Tanya,
PJ, Barbara, and
Aaron

A LETTER FROM SIX TEENAGERS

Chances are that eventually we'll all know someone who has AIDS. If you aren't having sex or using needles to inject drugs, you may think you don't have to know about AIDS. But everyone needs the facts. Like it or not, AIDS is part of our world. Experts say it's going to be around for a long time.

Maybe if you learn about AIDS you can help teach your friends, brothers or sisters, or parents about AIDS. Maybe you can prevent someone from getting infected with the AIDS virus.

The purpose of this book isn't to tell you what you should or shouldn't do. There are enough people in your life telling you that. This book will help you learn the facts about AIDS, how the AIDS virus is transmitted and how it's not. Then you can learn how to make decisions that will protect you from infection.

It's that simple. We call it the "information vaccine." If we get the facts and make decisions about our lives based on those facts, we are not likely to get AIDS.

Knowing about AIDS will help us make decisions. We might decide to wait to have sex. We might continue having sex but make it safer. Learning about people who became infected by injecting drugs may offer a new perspective on the dangers of drugs.

People of all ages, including teenagers, are getting infected with the AIDS virus. You don't have to be one of them.

RISKY TIMES

Chapter One
DENIAL

You might think you will live forever, that nothing bad can happen to you. That's normal. It's hard for someone young and healthy to imagine getting a serious illness that will never go away. But making it your business to know about AIDS may save your life.

Ali Gertz's story will help you understand that you could be at risk for AIDS.

Ali Gertz

THE STORY OF ALI GERTZ

Ali is curled up on her white Art Deco sofa. Her Pekingese dog, Sake, is snoozing on her lap. At first glance, Ali reminds you of a model on the cover of a magazine.

You would never guess by looking at Ali that she is nearly always exhausted.

Her body is frequently hot with fever. She's vulnerable to viruses that make her dizzy. And she is facing a probable slow, painful death. Ali has AIDS.

Ali tells stories about places she has traveled and people she has met. As the only child of a wealthy couple, Ali has lived a privileged life. She is decent, thoughtful, and fun to be with.

In high school Ali was one of the most popular girls in class. She had it all—brains, beauty, a big heart, and talent. She was an artist. A stack of drawings is tucked away in a big black leather portfolio on a drawing table next to the sofa. While she was still a teenager, Ali was admitted to one of the finest design schools in the country. After graduation she continued working hard to hone her skills. But her dreams of a successful career as an illustrator came crashing down the summer after she turned 23 when she became too tired and weak to draw.

"I was in the hospital for three weeks. I was so sick and I had a million painful tests. They couldn't find anything wrong with me. When I started to have trouble breathing, they took a biopsy of my lung. My doctor came into my room with tears in his eyes. He said, 'Ali, you have AIDS.' My first thought was 'My God! I am going to die!'"

Ali couldn't believe what she heard.

PJ: *"If we know the facts we can keep ourselves out of the range of AIDS. We can be AIDS–free and worry–free."*

Ben: *"I think as people learn about AIDS they will still be afraid but in a different way. I think it will change the way they look at AIDS. Rather than joke about it, they will learn the real risks. There are ways you can get AIDS and there are ways you can't, and you should know how to protect yourself."*

AIDS, in her mind, was a disease that afflicted gay men or intravenous drug users. She couldn't imagine how she had become infected. Finally, she traced it back seven years, to a handsome guy she knew when she was 16.

The guy worked as a bartender at a local club. They had a crush on each other and flirted with each other for a couple of years, and finally, they went out on a date. She remembers every detail of the night, including sex.

"It was a romantic evening, complete with candlelight, roses, and champagne. At that time I had suspicions that he might have been bisexual because many of the bartenders at that particular club were. That evening I remember asking him, 'Are you bisexual?' And he said no."

Ali knows now that he lied about his bisexuality. Even though he died from AIDS, Ali is positive he didn't know he was infected with the virus when they were together. Seven years ago most people had never heard of AIDS. Today, when so much is known about the disease, it can be prevented. No one has to suffer with AIDS.

"Teenagers have to stop thinking they are immortal and start thinking about being safe. Look, it happened to me, I was young and carefree and didn't think anything like this could happen to me."

Do you have a hard time believing what happened to Ali could happen to you? Do you think what happened to her was a fluke? It may be unusual, but doctors all over the country are reporting similar cases. If you put yourself at risk by engaging in certain behaviors, you too could get AIDS. If you don't believe that, you are kidding yourself.

Ali and Nancy

Nancy, Ali's Best Friend

When Nancy and Ali met in 1983, they felt as though they had known each other forever. Typical of best friends, they shared everything: their dreams, secrets, clothes, and tears. When Ali was diagnosed as having AIDS, Ali's mother called Nancy to the hospital.

"We all said nothing for five minutes, and we started to cry and hug each other. I am still in shock that she has AIDS. She has her bad days when she calls and says she is depressed and she wants to be normal and have babies. It breaks my heart. The other day she looked at me and said, 'Nan, I wish I would just die.' What do you say to that? I don't want her to die. I don't want to lose her."

Chapter Two
WHAT IS AIDS?

Aaron: *"It's hard enough to get straight information about sex and drugs. But AIDS is an avoided issue altogether, even though it's real serious. Look what it's doing. It's real dramatic. If you don't know anyone with it, you don't realize what AIDS can do. If you have the facts you will know what AIDS is and how to avoid it."*

AIDS stands for "acquired immune deficiency syndrome," a term that describes a condition that destroys the body's defenses against certain infections or cancers.

The disease is caused by a virus, which is a specific kind of germ. The name of the virus is HIV, which is an abbreviation for human immunodeficiency virus. HIV, the AIDS virus, gets inside certain cells in the body that make up a defense system called the immune system.

The immune system is in charge of attacking and destroying germs that enter the body. It protects us against illness and helps us recover once we get sick. Many different kinds of cells make up the immune system. Each type of cell performs a different job, although they all work together to protect the body from germs. The AIDS virus is deadly because it attacks and kills those cells in the immune system that help keep a person healthy. Those defender cells are called "helper T-cells." They have the important job of orchestrating many other parts of the immune response. Once the AIDS virus is inside the helper T-cells, the virus begins to multiply. The T-cells become miniature factories reproducing the AIDS virus. Eventually, the virus kills the cell. As more and more cells die, the immune system is less able to do its job. Infected people have a more difficult time fighting off germs, and so they develop infections.

You might think that if a person's immune system is damaged, he would get sick right away. But the AIDS virus destroys the T-cells slowly. The immune system can still do its job for a while even without all the T-cells. The body will suffer only after a certain number of cells are killed. How quickly someone develops symptoms after infection with the virus varies from person to person. Some people

"The tragedy of the AIDS virus is not exclusive to any one particular group. Its horrors touch us all, and the battle against this terrible disease must be the concern of everyone."
—Whitney Houston, *Singer*

Barbara: *"If we are aware of AIDS and we know the dangers of it and how it can be prevented, it will cut down on problems in the future. Right now, there is no cure for AIDS. The only way we can fight it is through education. So because of that—learn about it."*

become ill within weeks or months of infection. Others can be infected for 8 to 10 years, or even longer, before showing symptoms. Experts believe that in some people the virus is not very active in the cells until something—perhaps another infection—stimulates the AIDS virus to start multiplying. When the virus multiplies, it begins to kill the T-cells. Even then, the diagnosis might not be AIDS. Doctors speak of someone infected with the AIDS virus, called the Human Immunodeficiency Virus or HIV, as having HIV disease. The earliest symptoms may include infections of the skin or mouth; swollen glands; night sweats; fever and diarrhea. A person is diagnosed with AIDS only when he develops a drastic drop in the number of certain immune-system cells and more serious infections or cancer. The most common illnesses that signal AIDS are a type of pneumonia called Pneumocystis *carinii* pneumonia (PCP) and a cancer called Kaposi's sarcoma, which causes purple blotches or bumps on the skin.

No one is sure where the AIDS virus came from. Some experts believe it evolved in Africa more than 20 years ago and was brought to North America and Europe during the 1970s by people who had traveled to Africa. Some speculate that the virus lived in monkeys and eventually evolved so it could live in humans. But there is no documented proof of where AIDS originated. The first case of AIDS was diagnosed in the United States in 1981. Now the United States has more reported cases of AIDS than any other country in the world.

"I CAN NEVER GET AWAY FROM AIDS"

John, 23
Has AIDS

John is a good-looking guy, with the kind of face that people find attractive. John speaks loudly, quickly, and with confidence. But it's hard to concentrate on his words. You can't take your eyes away from the purple spot on the end of his nose. It is a symptom of Kaposi's sarcoma, an AIDS-related cancer. It is a constant reminder to John, and to everyone he meets, that he has AIDS.

"How would you like to look like this? I can never get away from the fact that I have AIDS. I notice people looking at my nose. They are so concerned about the fact that I have AIDS or that I might sneeze that they aren't listening to me."

It is frustrating for John that people can't hold a conversation with him. He has dedicated his life to developing his mind. While other kids played basketball and hockey, John read about French philosophy and European monarchies.

"I pushed myself hard. I took all advanced classes in school. I worked hard, got mostly A's in my classes so I could go to a good college. I always thought that improving my mind was important. It would allow me to get a better job, live in a nicer place."

Two courses short of graduation from New York University, John developed AIDS-related pneumonia. That is how he realized he had been infected with the AIDS virus through sex with another man. He recovered from the pneumonia, but for the past two years he has struggled with one infection after another—and Kaposi's sarcoma. The cancer on his nose faded a bit after radiation therapy, but his forehead, the roof of his mouth, his shoulders, and his right torso are still covered with purple blotches in various shapes and

"Get the facts!"

—Whoopi Goldberg,
Actress and comedienne

sizes. John can't predict where or when the next one will appear.

"I feel crummy almost every day. The things that I have wanted most in life are the things that are no longer available to me—like getting up in the morning, being able to go to a job and have a date and go out to dinner. That is really crushing."

John has lost some friends because of his disease. Even his mother is afraid. He moved back home, temporarily, after his diagnosis. In his own home, John felt like a leper.

Tanya: *"It's obvious why people should know about AIDS. If you know about AIDS you can make decisions based on the consequences of your spontaneous behavior."*

"One night, my mother and I were playing Scrabble. I sneezed all over the tiles and she swept them right up off the board and bleached them; then we started playing again. Every night before she went to bed, my mother bleached the toilet, sink, and bathtub. Then the next morning, she got up to take her shower first because she knew it was all clean. The thing that drove her crazy was if I used the bathroom in the morning first. Because then she would have to go through that bleaching routine again. It was very strange because she still hugs and kisses me. I don't know, that's just how she is. It made me feel horrible."

John knows his mother's illogical fears are shared by many people. He hopes that if people learn the facts about AIDS, they won't be so fearful.

Chapter Three

HOW YOU CAN AND CAN'T GET INFECTED

Hundreds of thousands of infected people have learned that HIV, the AIDS virus, doesn't care whom it infects. It does not discriminate. It is passed from person to person. Outside the body the virus is weak; inside the body it is strong. The virus will live in anyone who gives it a chance by exposing himself or herself to it. The AIDS virus is found in blood, in the fluids in the vagina, in semen, and in the fluids that leak from a man's penis before an orgasm.

HOW AIDS IS SPREAD

Vaginal sex: When a man puts his penis into a woman's vagina, it's called vaginal sex. It's the most common kind of sex between men and women. If the man is infected with the AIDS virus, the fluids from his penis can get into the woman's bloodstream through a tear in the vagina that may be so small it can't be felt or seen. Or it may be possible for the AIDS virus to get into the blood through certain cells lining the vagina. Though the first cases of AIDS in this country were reported among gay men, about 12% of all AIDS cases in the United States are now among women. In Africa, there are equal numbers of men and women who have AIDS. Experts predict that the number of women with AIDS in the United States will increase as the virus spreads among heterosexual drug users and their sex partners.

Alexei: *"It's important that kids and grownups not be afraid of AIDS and that they know how to protect themselves from it and cope with it. If we know about AIDS, we will be able to interact with people who have AIDS and try to help them, not exclude them."*

Anal sex: When a man puts his penis into his sex partner's anus it's called anal sex. The skin of the rectum is especially tender and can easily tear during anal sex. When this happens, the fluids from his penis may get through the skin of the rectum and into the bloodstream. Some doctors say it is also possible for the virus to infect certain cells directly in the lining of the rectum. So even if the skin doesn't tear, infection with the virus can occur. Infection can pass the other way, too: the rectum can bleed if irritated by the penis, letting infected blood into the body through the penis. Whether you are a man or a woman, anal intercourse is risky.

Oral sex: Contact between a person's genitals and a sex partner's mouth is oral sex. Virus in the fluids of the penis or the vagina can get into the body through cuts or openings in the mouth. Scientists do not know whether HIV can enter your bloodstream through your digestive tract if swallowed.

Kissing: The AIDS virus has been found in small amounts in the saliva of some people, but researchers have never found AIDS to be spread by kissing. Scientists say there just isn't enough virus in saliva to cause infection. Experts believe that if an infected person, with even a small open cut in his mouth or on his lips, kisses someone who also has a cut in the mouth, the virus could be passed in infected blood. But most scientists agree you can enjoy kissing without worrying about AIDS transmission.

Shooting drugs intravenously (into your veins): When people inject drugs, they also draw their blood into the needle and syringe (the hollow cartridge that holds the needle). If other people use that needle and syringe without first cleaning it, they can be exposed to the blood in the needle and syringe. If the blood contains HIV, then the virus will also be injected when the next person shoots up. It is likely that infection will occur.

Tattoos, ear piercing, and shooting steroids: If you share a needle with another person for any of these activities, you are risking possible infection with the AIDS virus because the needle you share could

"If you truly want to win the competition, do it clean. If you use steroids, every time you inject, you risk infection with the AIDS virus. Besides, if you are on steroids, your face blows up like a pumpkin, and you look ugly as hell. People will laugh at you."

—Jesse "The Bod" Ventura,
Food and Drug Administration's national spokesman on steroids, actor, former professional wrestler

be contaminated with infected blood. If you get a tattoo or pierced ears by a professional who uses a sterile needle for each customer, there is no risk of infection with HIV, the AIDS virus.

If you shoot steroids with a sterile needle, there is no threat of infection with the AIDS virus, though oral or injected steroids pose many other serious health risks. Steroids are dangerous drugs. If you use them to make yourself stronger or faster for competitive sports, or to look better, you're definitely risking your life.

Transfusions: When you receive blood because of an accident or illness, it is called a transfusion. Because HIV is found in blood, a transfusion of an infected person's blood into your body is another way the AIDS virus can be spread. All blood in the United States is now tested for the AIDS virus *before* it is given to another person, but this was not always the case. Before the test was available, thousands of people were infected with the virus through blood products. The test has made blood products safer but there is still a small risk of infection because no test is 100% accurate. Also, some people may donate blood so soon after they have become infected that signs of the infection may not show up on the test.

Anyone planning to have surgery that might require a blood transfusion should consider autologous donation, which is a process by which you donate and store your own blood over a 4- to 6-week period before surgery. This is primarily recommended to avoid infection with the hepatitis virus, but it will also help avoid infection with HIV. Many hospitals now offer this option to patients. You may get more information from your doctor's office, health center, or clinic.

Hemophilia: Hemophiliacs are people who lack a clotting substance in their blood. They can control their disorder through frequent infusions of a clotting factor, called anti-hemophilic factor (AHF). AHF is made by pooling thousands of units of blood plasma, which is the clear, liquid portion of the blood.

Before blood testing for the presence of HIV, the AIDS virus, began in 1985, thousands of hemophiliacs became infected by receiving AHF contaminated with the AIDS virus. AHF, which had proved to be a lifesaver for hemophiliacs, became a potential killer.

Across the country between 96% and 98% of all hemophiliacs—about 20,000 people—are infected with the AIDS virus as a result of treatment for their disorder.

Ben: *"The fact of the matter is it can happen to you. You have to be smart enough to admit AIDS is a real danger, a possibility no matter how remote, a risk that is not worth taking. No matter how you try to rationalize it away, it can happen."*

Accidental exposure to blood or body fluids: A small number of doctors, researchers, nurses, and other health-care workers have been infected with the AIDS virus by caring for people with AIDS or by working with infected blood products. In each case, they were either splashed with large amounts of infected blood or stuck by needles while drawing blood from an infected person. Although these accidents are not rare, they usually don't result in infection.

Transmission from a pregnant woman to her unborn child: If a woman is infected with the AIDS virus, there is a significant chance the virus will be passed on to her unborn child, either in the womb or during birth. Studies now suggest there is a 35% chance of this occurring. Further studies are underway. For complex biological reasons, some babies are born with just the mother's antibodies to the AIDS virus, not the virus itself. In those babies, after about one year the antibodies will disappear. Until then, evidence of antibodies will show up on tests, and it will appear the baby has been infected with the AIDS virus. There are also reports of babies being infected while breast-feeding from an infected mother.

A HEMOPHILIAC'S STORY

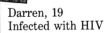

Darren, 19
Infected with HIV

Darren is a hemophiliac who has been exposed to the AIDS virus. He hasn't developed any symptoms of AIDS, but his infection has shaken his life. Soon after his 16th birthday, Darren appeared on a television newscast and talked about his infection with the AIDS virus. His boss at a fast-food restaurant saw the interview and fired him.

"I was mad. Who was he to tell me I can't work? I did my job. I didn't do anything wrong. He never told me I couldn't come in there and eat. He just said I couldn't work there. What's the difference between punching buttons on his cash registers and sitting at one of his booths?"

When Darren and his family threatened to take the restaurant owner to court, Darren was allowed back to work.

But that wasn't the end of Darren's troubles. He and his girlfriend were enrolled in the same college, and late one night she called him from her dorm, sobbing.

"My girlfriend said she didn't want to go out with me anymore. She said stuff was being said about me, that I had AIDS. And some of her roommates didn't want to stay with her in the dorm anymore. They were mad because I used their bathroom and shower."

Darren was upset that his girlfriend was having a hard time. She had stayed with him through so much. So Darren dealt with the problem head-on. He met with her roommates and explained to them how you can and can't get infected with the AIDS virus. He assured them they were not in danger just because he had used their shower. Some of the room-

"Our society is afflicted by a deadly virus that has plagued our generation and caused many deaths: AIDS! Passed on through unprotected sex and drug abuse, it can affect all of us.

Lack of knowledge can be your worst enemy. Don't be afraid or embarrassed to ask questions about AIDS. It could save your life!"

—Bobby Brown, *Singer*

mates believed him. But two of the girls couldn't overcome their fear and moved out. Darren's girlfriend stuck by him.

"What's really aggravating is that I didn't have a choice about being exposed to this disease. It happened and I had no choice. Today, kids have a choice. They can protect themselves. Use a condom. You might be embarrassed, but use it anyway."

"IT HURTS MY HEART"

Darlene, 35
Her son, Jeremy, 3
Both have AIDS

You can look at Darlene and know her life has been tough. Years of drug abuse have left scars on her body, dark circles under her eyes, and the AIDS virus in her blood. Darlene became infected by shooting drugs with a needle contaminated by the AIDS virus. That was before her son, Jeremy, was born. Now he has AIDS, too. He got it from his mother. Darlene is tormented by the knowledge that her son will die because she shared needles.

"My son gets sores on his head, his

arms, and his ears. I feel guilty because of what I have done. I shot dope and cocaine and I had sex with people and I gave AIDS to my boy. It hurts. Believe me, it hurts my heart. My son is going to die. There's nothing I can do about it. I love him dearly. All I can say is, don't have sex without protecting yourself. And don't use a needle."

A girl or woman who thinks she might be infected should *not* risk becoming pregnant before being tested to determine whether she has been exposed to the AIDS virus.

Carolyn, 23
Infected with HIV

A FAMILY FIGHTS TO STAY WELL

Carolyn looks remarkably healthy. Her skin is reddened from an afternoon at the beach. Her teeth are white and straight. She is strong and confident as she poses for a photograph in the office of the AIDS Action Committee of Boston. Carolyn and about 50 other people infected with the AIDS virus have just finished their weekly dinner meeting. It's their chance to get together and talk. Carolyn's friends here refer to her as "the gorgeous one."

In high school, Carolyn had "tons of friends." They understood that she had little time to party. She was a disciplined dancer. Jazz and tap-dancing lessons after school and ballet every Saturday absorbed most of her time. And there was Karl. Karl was Carolyn's love. She met and started dating Karl when she was 13. "He was totally wild and crazy. He was the kind of guy who would think nothing of walking down the grocery store aisle and suddenly starting to dance. He was so spontaneous. I loved him a lot."

Barbara: *"It doesn't matter if you are healthy or not, male or female—anyone can get AIDS."*

Carolyn and Karl were together six years. They shared everything. At least Carolyn thought so. But Karl had a secret. He was bisexual. One day Karl became violently ill and had to be hospitalized. A month later, he was dead.

"He had been sick through the whole summer. He was tired and cranky and had lost a lot of weight. He just wasn't himself at all. When he went into the hospital, he was diagnosed with AIDS. And then everything happened so fast."

Carolyn knew there was a good chance she had become infected during sexual intercourse with Karl. So she got tested and found out she *was* infected.

"I didn't want to deal with it. It took a while before I could accept my diagnosis. I was in total shock; I was devastated. I have heard young people say you can tell when someone has AIDS, but I know you can't—not even if it's someone you have been with for a long time. There could be skeletons in the closet they won't want to tell you about."

Carolyn was afraid she would never fall in love again. At a time when she needed support, some of her closest friends would have nothing to do with her.

"I took a week off from my job for Karl's funeral, and the morning I was supposed to go back, they called and said they didn't need me anymore. People with AIDS deserve to be treated with respect. You can't get AIDS by touching me or hugging me or talking to me. One of the worst things is to be so young and find out you have a life-threatening disease and be rejected by people because of it."

But Carolyn was not alone for long. Roy, an old boyfriend, came back into her life. He was stable and secure, just what Carolyn wanted. They dated, fell in love again, and got married. When they made love, Carolyn asked Roy to use condoms to protect himself from infection. He didn't think it was necessary. He was wrong. He did get infected.

Roy, 25
Infected with the
AIDS virus

"A lot of people think AIDS is just a gay people's disease, and it's not. It happened to me. I slept with a woman, not a man. Everyone should use protection. You can't take a chance because you just don't know."

Roy and Carolyn are fighting to stay well. They eat healthfully and try to reduce the stress in their lives through meditation. Some days Carolyn is so tired, she struggles to stay awake until Roy comes home from work at five o'clock. Even when she doesn't feel well, she reminds herself that life is precious.

"Living with AIDS is learning to live. I have to learn to enjoy each day and make the best out of it because I don't know what is down the road for me."

Carolyn has another reason to fight so hard to live. She and Karl had a baby. He is young and needs his mommy. He was born to Carolyn before she realized she was infected with the AIDS virus. He, too, is infected with the AIDS virus. Once people are infected, they remain infected forever. And they are capable of infecting others, as the story of Carolyn and Roy proves.

Carolyn died in November, 1989, after developing pneumocystis pneumonia.

HOW AIDS CAN BE SPREAD

Peter and Paula meet and decide they want to have sex.

Peter   *Paula*

Paula has heard of AIDS, but thinks Peter is a good-looking guy and seems nice. He couldn't be infected with any sexually transmitted diseases, she thinks. He certainly *looks* healthy.

But Paula isn't looking at the big picture. She is not considering that in the past Peter may have slept with someone who had been exposed to infection.

To help you understand, consider this:

Peter's former girlfriend is Diane. Peter and Diane had sex. Diane had sex with two guys, Chuck and Jon, before she had sex with Peter.

Chuck's three partners before Diane were Patti, Deanna, and Judy. Jon's old girlfriend was Betty.

Deanna had had sex with one person, Jason, before Chuck. Jason's former partner had been Janet.

Judy's first partner was Scott.

Betty had two previous sexual relationships, with Tom and Kevin, who was bisexual and involved with Jack.

So when Paula says she is safe with Peter, she is for-

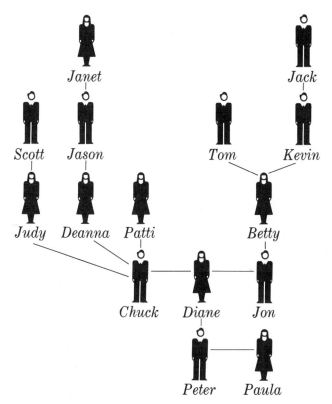

getting about the other *13 people* in the picture. If any one of those people is infected, HIV could have been spread. For instance, Scott could be infected and not know it. So remember: When you sleep with someone, in a way you are having sex with all his or her previous partners.

A man or woman, adult or teenager, could be infected with the AIDS virus for many years *without knowing it,* and could unwittingly infect a lot of people. Former U.S. Surgeon General C. Everett Koop has said that when you sleep with a person, in essence, you sleep with all his or her previous sex partners. The illustration on the preceding pages will help you understand that concept.

Barbara, 23
Infected with the
AIDS virus

"HE NEVER TOLD ME"

Barbara and Alice sit at the kitchen table, smoking cigarettes and telling one story after another. It's a familiar scene in their small, old country house. By the way they carry on, you might think they were sisters instead of mother and daughter. It's been that way since Barbara's mother and father were divorced when she was seven.

"I was old enough during my mother and father's divorce that my mom could talk to me. I was always there for her. We talked about everything. We were like best friends." Now, 15 years later, Barbara's mother is there for her.

In the summer of 1988, Barbara was engaged to be married. She and her fiancé were touring cross-country when Barbara became pregnant. Excited about the prospect of becoming parents, they returned home to plan their wedding. Two weeks later, the doctor who gave Barbara her pregnancy test called with bad news. Additional tests showed she was infected with HIV. Barbara was stunned. She didn't even know the doctor was testing her for presence of the AIDS virus. Why would he test her for AIDS? After all, she thought only homosexuals and intravenous drug users were at risk for AIDS. She wasn't gay and had never used needles. She didn't think she could get AIDS. What Barbara didn't know was that her fiancé had shared needles to shoot drugs several years before they met.

"I heard about AIDS on TV. But everything I heard went in one ear and out the other. When I realized you could get AIDS through sex, I didn't worry. I had been faithful to Steve for three years. I always said I was happy I was with one person. I used to feel so bad for these kids who were out dating around. I had no idea Steve had used needles. He never told me."

Imagine what it was like for Barbara. She was planning her wedding. She was thrilled at the prospect of being a mother. Everything she had wanted in life seemed within her grasp. Then suddenly it was all gone. Barbara and her fiancé split up. After much agonizing, she had an abortion. At the age of 22, she was facing the possibility of a painful death. Now Barbara is afraid she will never see her dreams come true.

"It's always been important to me to get married and have children and be in love. You know, the house with the picket fence. I can get a job and go on with my life, but there is such a big part of my life missing. It's a scary feeling."

When Barbara became infected, she knew almost nothing about AIDS. Today, that's not the case. Barbara wants to help young people learn about AIDS so they can protect themselves against it.

"It's not just IV drug users and gays. You have to treat everyone as if they were infected. If someone you want to have sex with gets upset about it, so what? You have to take care of yourself, because if you don't there is always a chance you will get infected. You might even want to wait until you are married to have sex. I wish I could go back and be 16 and know all this. I wouldn't be so anxious to fit in and please a man. I wouldn't be in this fix today if I had stood up for myself."

Alice, Barbara's mother

When Barbara told her family she was infected with the AIDS virus, her mother, Alice, had a strong reaction.

"I behaved very ugly. I don't have a habit of swearing, but I swore. I wanted to throw something. I didn't know how to deal with it at that moment. Also, I wanted to protect her. It was like, how can I deal with it and help her at the same time? I hugged her and kissed her, naturally, and said we are going to beat this, you are going to beat this and live."

One night, when Barbara and her mother were out to dinner, it all came to a head.

"We were out having pizza and I couldn't hack it. I started crying at the pizza parlor. I told her, 'I know I have to accept that you might die. I will hold you and be with you right to the end.' We both broke down and were crying in each other's arms. We ended up that night praying on our knees together. That helped both of us tremendously."

Barbara's mother pays close attention to news of AIDS treatment developments. She has not given up hope that a miracle will save her daughter.

Chapter Four
CONDOMS

Condom: A thin latex rubber cover for the penis. A tip at the end of the condom catches semen when a man has an orgasm.

Maybe you think condoms make great water balloons but you can't imagine using one during sex. Before you reject the idea altogether, read this chapter. It could save your life. Remember, by actions you take, *you control* whether you get AIDS or any other sexually transmitted diseases.

If you have sex with anyone you are not absolutely sure is infection–free—and that's almost impossible to know—condoms are a must.

Many teenagers are choosing to wait until they are older before having sex—and there are plenty of reasons to wait. But some teenagers are having sex now, and if you are one of them, you don't want to get sick in the process. The only way you can be 100% certain that you won't become infected with the AIDS virus through sex is by abstaining from sex. If you do decide to have sex, however, condoms will make it a lot safer for both of

Ali: *"If there is a chemistry between two people and they want to be together badly enough they will use condoms. Condoms don't have to be a romance breaker. There are sexy ways to use condoms. If two people really care about each other, they will use condoms."*

you. They will help you avoid direct contact with semen that may contain the AIDS virus. They also offer protection from contact with vaginal fluids that may contain the virus. So use your brain—use a condom!

It's true, HIV is not the only reason to use protection during intercourse. Condoms can help prevent pregnancy and more than 30 sexually transmitted diseases, including syphilis, gonorrhea, herpes, chancroid, genital warts, chlamydia, and trichomoniasis. A person can have a sexually transmitted disease without showing symptoms. Left untreated, some of these can cause serious health problems, including sterility (the inability to have children). Anyone having unprotected sex is at risk for sexually transmitted diseases, and statistics show that teenagers are becoming infected at an

"Some people equate having to partake in safer sex with losing freedom. By using condoms, you know, you are not losing freedom, you are protecting your life.

—Susan Dey, *Actress*

Ben: *"If you are a guy, you take care of it, you know what I am saying? If you are a girl you should insist on it no matter what. Don't be embarrassed."*

PJ: *"Don't be a jerk. Use a condom. Some girls might want to impress a guy so much that they don't ask him to use a condom. That's not impressive, that's stupid."*

alarming rate: every year, 1 in every 6 sexually active teenagers contracts a sexually transmitted disease.

Health experts say that some sexually transmitted diseases (such as genital herpes and syphilis) cause breaks or lesions in the skin that may make it easier for the AIDS virus to get into the body during sexual intercourse. In any case, for maximum protection with condoms, you must use one *every time* you have sex. Just thinking about using a condom doesn't count. Having a condom in your pocket and not using it during sex doesn't count. Using condoms 9 out of 10 times is better than not using them at all, but what if you get infected with the AIDS virus that one time you don't use a condom? It makes *no sense* to have sex without protection.

If you are tempted to avoid using a condom by asking your partner if he or she is "safe," remember: Chances are your partner doesn't know. Your partner may give you what he or she thinks is an honest answer. But the fact is he or she may not really know. And some people are so anxious to make a good impression, they won't tell the truth. Do you have a hard time believing someone you are attracted to would lie to you? You can't be sure, so be safe. Use condoms.

Some guys say the reason they don't

want to use condoms is that they've heard condoms can dull the feeling of sex. But millions of people do use condoms. Condoms are now made to be effective without lessening sensitivity. Sex still feels great, even with a condom. And there's much more to it than intercourse. If your only alternative is risking infection with a deadly virus, doesn't it seem smart to use condoms?

Alexei: *"You don't want to mess with your life. If he isn't going to put on a condom, forget it."*

Deciding you will use condoms is the first step. The next step, probably the hardest step, is to talk with your partner about your decision. That thought may make you cringe. You may think, "Oh, I'll bring up the subject next time." But the next time might be too late.

Many people feel nervous about discussing the use of condoms with a possible sex partner. Some might be afraid the guy or girl will lose interest in them. But people are becoming more aware of AIDS and the importance of protecting themselves. Talking about condoms may be a lot easier

"For me it just took one time. I am living proof it can happen the first time. Don't be suicidal, use condoms."

—Ali Gertz

METHODS OF BIRTH CONTROL

Diaphragm: A diaphragm is a small rubber disk that holds contraceptive jelly or cream and covers the cervix. A girl must be measured so that the doctor can prescribe the right size diaphragm. A proper fit is important for the prevention of pregnancy. The diaphragm can be put in several hours before intercourse. After intercourse, it must be left in for six to eight hours. The diaphragm works by acting as a barrier to prevent sperm from entering the uterus and by holding the jelly or cream against the cervix, thereby killing any sperm that manage to swim around the rim of the diaphragm. When used properly, the diaphragm is 80 to 90% effective in preventing pregnancy.

Cervical Cap: Like a diaphragm, a cervical cap covers the cervix and must be fitted by a doctor. The cap can be left in for several days. Properly used, it is 80 to 90% effective in preventing pregnancy. The cervical cap is new and not yet widely available. But some family-planning clinics do offer this form of birth control.

Sponge: The contraceptive foam sponge is treated with spermicide and covers the cervix. It can be inserted up to 24 hours before sex. The sponge works three ways: by releasing a spermicide, absorbing sperm, and blocking the cervix to prevent sperm from entering the uterus. You can purchase a contraceptive sponge in most drugstores and do not need a doctor's prescription. If used properly the sponge is 90% effective in preventing pregnancy.

IUD: An IUD (intrauterine device) is a small piece of plastic that a doctor inserts inside the uterus. It is a very effective means of birth control (97 to 98%). Doctors say the IUD probably works by preventing implantation of the fertilized egg. The major risk associated with IUD use is a serious infection of the pelvic organs that in some cases can cause infertility, or the inability to bear children.

The Pill: The birth control pill contains synthetic hormones estrogen and progesterone, which suppress the natural hormone cycle, preventing the release of the egg. If the female doesn't release an egg, pregnancy cannot occur. When used properly, the Pill is 99% effective in preventing pregnancy.

Contraceptive Foam: Contraceptive foam is inserted into the vagina with a syringe-like applicator, as close to the cervix as possible. The foam, which contains the spermicide nonoxynol-9, works by killing sperm and by keeping sperm out of the uterus. Though foam loses its full effectiveness about an hour after it is inserted, it should not be washed out for 6–8 hours after intercourse. Used alone, foam is only about 80% effective in preventing pregnancy because it's often used improperly. But if you follow instructions carefully, foam can be an effective contraceptive. Doctors say foam, used with a condom, can be 95% effective in preventing pregnancy.

Ben: *"What if a girl says, 'You don't need a condom, I am on the pill'?"*

PJ: *"I'd wonder how many guys she said that to before. It seems that comment would be a hint that a guy should be careful!"*

than you think. And your partner may be relieved you raised the subject so he or she didn't have to.

Once you are aroused and become intimate with someone, it can be awkward and difficult to stop to discuss protection. Plan to bring the subject up ahead of time. Waiting until you are in the heat of passion can be dangerous. Sexual feelings are powerful. You may find yourself giving in to those feelings and putting yourself at risk. Remember, one careless action could cost you your life.

Some of you will feel too shy to talk about having sex ahead of time. Or you and your partner may move faster than you anticipated and suddenly, without any planning, you want to have sex. You can try to avoid that, but it makes sense to be prepared. Carry a condom in your wallet or your purse. Each partner is *equally responsible* for using protection during sex. You should not rely on other people to look out for you; be ready to protect *yourself*. This means carrying a condom, just in case.

Condoms are disease-transmission control as well as birth control. Since neither the diaphragm nor the Pill will protect you from disease (because neither can keep semen from coming into contact with the skin of the vagina), it's important to use a condom every time you have sex. Be-

HOW TO USE A CONDOM

It might be awkward to put on a condom the first time, so boys might want to practice some of these steps privately.

1. Open the package only when you are ready to use it. Air, heat, and light can spoil latex condoms. When you are opening the package, be careful not to tear the condom. If you are excited and in a hurry, the package can be hard to open.

2. Squeeze the tip of the condom so there is no air trapped in the end. This is important so there is room for the semen during ejaculation.

3. Put the condom on the end of the penis and roll it onto the erect penis. (Remember to hold on to the tip of the condom until it's on all the way.)

4. If you want to use a lubricant, make sure to use one that is *water-based* (such as K-Y Jelly or Ramses Lubricating). Do not use oil-based lubricants such as petroleum jelly, mineral oil, vegetable oil, or cold cream. Oil-based lubricants weaken the latex in a condom, making it more likely to break.

5. After ejaculation, hold on to the condom at the rim and pull out while your penis is still hard. If you wait until the penis is soft, the condom can slip off and semen can spill out.

6. Throw the condom away. You can use it only once.

cause condoms can break or leak, doctors advise using additional birth control (the diaphragm, the Pill, foam, or the sponge) to avoid pregnancy.

HOW TO GET A CONDOM

Once you have decided that you want to have sex, it's time to get condoms. Many health clinics offer them for free. Or you can buy them at any pharmacy or convenience store. Anyone can buy them, young or old, male or female. There is an endless variety of condoms. Some are advertised as form-fitting and no-slip. Others are ribbed for extra sensation. There are many different colors and textures. Some condoms cost more than others. Be sure to buy condoms made of *latex*, a type of rubber material, rather than animal skin. This should be clearly

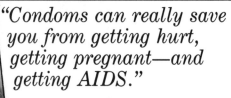

"Condoms can really save you from getting hurt, getting pregnant—and getting AIDS."

—Steve Tyler, *Aerosmith*

HOW TO TALK TO YOUR PARTNER ABOUT CONDOMS

If the idea of talking about condoms with a potential sex partner makes you nervous, you might practice with the following phrases. Some of these lines might not be right for you, but they could help you find the right ones.

"If this isn't important to you—if it doesn't mean enough to you that you wear a condom—then forget it."

"If you don't respect me enough to understand that this is important, then obviously I'm with the wrong person."

"Not if we're not safe."

"Look, without a condom I'm not going to do it. That's the way it is."

"This isn't a joke. This means something to me. It's important to protect ourselves."

"If you care, if it means something, you'll use a condom."

"It protects both of us—this is just as much for you as it is for me."

"I have to get a condom—it'll only take a second."

"If you can't even talk about it, maybe we aren't ready to do this."

written on the box. Latex condoms are stronger than those made out of animal skin so they are less likely to break or leak. Also look for condoms treated with nonoxynol-9, which is known to kill the AIDS virus.

It is perfectly normal to be nervous about buying condoms the first time.

Alan Kramer, Pharmacist

"A lot of people are shy when it comes to asking for condoms. I have a son and a daughter, and I hope that when and if they decide to have sex, they would feel comfortable enough to buy condoms. I want to stress to them that pregnancy is certainly one concern of having sex, but AIDS and other diseases are equally if not more serious. I would explain to them, 'Your mother and father have tried to teach you responsibility. If you decide to have sex, this [using condoms] is something we want you to do for your protection, because we love you.' I think many kids are going to have sex anyway, so it's important for them to be safe. At my pharmacy I see kids 13 and 14 coming in pregnant. I also see a number of AIDS patients here, too. When someone comes in to buy condoms, my attitude is, without exception, 'Here is someone who is taking responsibility for his own actions.' I think most pharmacists feel that way."

If you decide to have sex and are buying condoms from a person you feel is judgmental, buy them in a different store and remember that you're right to be cautious and safe when having sex.

For condoms to be as effective as possible, it's important that you use them correctly. Condoms are put on before you begin to have intercourse, when the penis is erect, or hard. Fluids that leak out of the penis before an orgasm and a girl's fluids that lubricate the vagina can both contain HIV, the AIDS virus.

If you carry condoms in your purse or your wallet, be aware that heat can damage them and they might break more easily. It's always a good idea to have a condom tucked away, but if you carry it for more than a few months without using it, throw it out and store a new one. Condoms are made stronger and better than ever, but this is no guarantee they won't break. Studies show they tend to break more frequently during anal intercourse than vaginal intercourse. So when making a decision about what kind of sex you will have, keep that in mind.

Ben: *"The first time I bought condoms I was so scared. I wondered, 'Are they going to call my mom?' I went into the store, walked up to the shelf, and grabbed the box. I didn't stand there looking too long. There were two cash registers. A man was at one, a woman at another. Of course the woman's register came up first. I felt so self-conscious and idiotic, but it was all over in a second. I put them down, and she looked at me with this stoic face and rang them up and put them in a bag, and I ran out of that store really fast!"*

RELIGIOUS VIEWS

Some young people may have conflicting feelings about using condoms because of their religious upbringing. Some leaders in the Catholic church, for example, object to the use of condoms because they are a form of birth control, which the church officially opposes. Others consider birth control a morally right and responsible practice. And many public-health officials consider condoms disease-transmission control, not just birth control.

Father Ted Brown, Catholic Priest and Campus Minister

66 **A**ccording to the Catholic church, the only morally acceptable way to avoid AIDS is to abstain from sexual acts before marriage and to refrain from shooting drugs.

"This may be easier for some to do than for others. AIDS is a complex issue, and being a teenager isn't always easy.

"So staying healthy means more than *not* doing something. It actually means doing a lot of things. It means reaching down into yourselves and believing that you are good and your lives are worth saving. With all the pressures of being a

Alexei: *"I think sex is something special, and I think there is a certain closeness you have to have that you shouldn't push. I want to enjoy it and not feel tense about the whole thing. I am glad about how things have gone for me. I haven't succumbed to any pressure from anybody."*

teenager—building relationships and exploring who you are as young adults—that can be a challenge. But good friends, loving parents, a teacher, a member of the clergy, or another trusted adult can help you see your worth. If you are feeling good about yourselves, you are more likely to make healthy decisions.

"If you do not accept the Church's teaching and become sexually active before marriage, it is important to follow the advice of health-care experts."

The Reverend Jennifer Philips, Episcopalian Priest

PJ: *"You should only do it when you want to, only if you want to. If you don't want to do it, it's a waste, especially if it's your first time. You should really, really like someone—then it means something, not just a romp in the hay to have a notch on your belt."*

"**T**hink of yourself as a person deserving love, care, and respect, and think of those around you in the same way. When it comes to sexuality, respect means not putting pressure on each other to have sex—or to be other than the way you are. Taking care means not taking chances with health and safety. If you have sex, use a condom every time whether you are gay or straight. Rubbers help protect against venereal disease, pregnancy, and AIDS. I believe that sexuality is God's gift—as is the body—and what we do with it affects our whole being—physical, mental, and spiritual. It's too important to treat carelessly or casually. Making wise and careful choices about sexuality is good for the spirit and, in this age of AIDS, it can also save your life and the lives of the people with whom you are intimate.

"I was embarrassed the first time I bought condoms. I must have walked around the drugstore three times before I went up to the counter to ask for them, and I picked a drugstore where I'd never been before. Then I worried that my partner would think I was a jerk. But I cared enough for him and for myself that I wanted to keep us both healthy and myself not pregnant. And I thought about becoming sexually active long and carefully beforehand. It turned out that when we finally made the decision, he had bought condoms, too—he had wanted to take care of me and himself and wanted our relationship to last."

Rabbi Herman Blumberg

"**M**y favorite expression when talking to young people today is 'Take care.' Take care, I say, when you are driving a car, when you are eating, when you have the opportunity to do drugs or alcohol. And in the 1990s, *take care* when sexually involved with anyone.

"My religion, Judaism, asks me to take care of my body because it is precious and delicate, a gift from God. What does this

PJ: *"When a girl brings up the subject of protection, some guys might say, 'Do you think I have a disease? Or I am gay?' "*

have to do with sex? Sex can be great when it is an expression of love. Sex is wonderful when partners are equally willing and ready. Sex can be stupendous when it reflects an ongoing relationship. Sex can be even better than that when it is part of a good, lasting marriage.

"But sex can be ugly when one partner is unwilling, coerced, or forced. Sex can be destructive when a person is used and discarded like an empty soda can. Sex can be deadly when it leaves people with diseases, the most deadly of which is AIDS!

"Sex is good when you are really ready. Otherwise, say no. Don't be pushed. If sex is right for you (it is *not* right for everyone by a particular age) then take care. In this day and age this includes using a condom to protect yourself against diseases, particularly AIDS.

"When young people ask me if Judaism says it's okay to use condoms, I reply, Judaism says that if you are having sex you should use condoms. Judaism says, 'Take care.'"

NO PEACE AT HOME

Alin has a bright outlook on life. And when you think about all he's been through, that's amazing. As a youngster, Alin was constantly hassled by other

Barbara: *"I'd say that I'd feel more comfortable using condoms even though I believe him when he says he doesn't have a disease. I would just tell him it's safer—and not just for AIDS, but to protect against other diseases and also pregnancy. It's something I have thought about and it's a decision I have made. If I am going to sleep with someone, I hope he will respect that."*

Alin, 38
Infected with
the AIDS virus

kids. Neighborhood bullies made fun of him because he had a black mother and a white father.

"Life was pretty tough. I wasn't considered black and I wasn't considered white. I kept getting beat up and having things taken from me—books, money."

Alin found little peace at home. He never knew his real father. His stepfather drank and then beat up him and his mother. Alin tried to defend them but he wasn't big or strong enough. After years of abuse, at the age of 18, Alin left home. He earned money working as a bartender and moving furniture. Alin made lots of friends and his social life picked up. But as winter came, Alin got sick. An infection festered in his throat and stomach. His doctor treated the illness and tested Alin for presence of HIV, the AIDS virus. He had heard about AIDS a couple of years ago and had started practicing safer sex, but by then he was already infected.

Alin figures sexually active young adults, by the choices they make, have a chance to live infection-free.

"If you want to say no, say no! But if you are going to have sex, use a condom. AIDS is too much of a risk to take. You could say, 'This one time it's not going to happen.' Well that's gambling. It could boil down to that one time because that's all it takes to get infected."

INSTEAD OF INTERCOURSE

Sex is more than "doing it." Your whole body can be affected by a touch, a kiss, a feeling of intimacy. With imagination you can feel good and still be safe.

Tanya: There are tons of things you can do instead of intercourse. Be creative. You can kiss and mess around and feel each other—you know, flesh rubbing up against flesh, without having intercourse. Massaging is great—even if it's just your feet! You can feel closer to a person because it's not just physical—a long, quiet talk can bring you worlds closer than intercourse can.

Ben: What you do depends on what you are comfortable with. There *are* plenty of options.

Barbara: If you want to be intimate with someone, you can kiss, cuddle, even flirt. Heavy petting can be as fulfilling as intercourse without taking as many risks.

Aaron: You can mess around and get aroused without intercourse. And it's safer, emotionally and physically.

Alexei: In some cases fooling around is better because you may think you are ready for intercourse but you're really just looking for closeness.

PJ: You could do a lot of snuggling with music, poetry, and hugs. You can get into heavy petting and mutual masturbation. You don't have to have intercourse to show that you want to be close to someone. Sex is a big step and and lots of kids aren't ready for it. So hanging around and being close can be just right.

Chapter Five
DECISIONS

It's normal to be afraid of getting AIDS. But remember, you determine whether you get infected by the decisions you make and the actions you take. The AIDS virus is not lurking around every corner waiting to attack. Choices you make can either put you at risk of infection or help protect you from it.

When you are a teenager, it seems that people are always telling you how to run your life. You follow orders all day long: Don't be late for school. Do your homework. Don't shout. Drive slowly. Don't do drugs. Don't stay out late.

Sometimes you probably feel that you have no control over your own life. But from the time you get up in the morning until you put your head on your pillow at night, you make hundreds of your own decisions. Think back on today. After you got out of bed, you made a decision about what clothes you would wear. From socks to shirts, you made a half-dozen decisions. Did you decide to eat breakfast or skip it? How about picking out a route to school, or whether to stop by your locker on the way to class? See? Every minute of every

PJ: *"If you think the people you are hanging around with will like you more if you have sex, then maybe you should find some new friends. Find some who can like you just the way you are."*

day you are making choices. Sometimes you decide to do things that are risky. That's a part of being a teenager. You might drive a car at high speeds, or chain-smoke cigarettes without worrying about the consequences. Maybe you rationalize by telling yourself nothing bad can happen to someone so young. At this time in your life, you are reaching out to explore the world and, at times, pushing the limits. Sometimes you do that without considering the price you may have to pay. There have always been consequences of unprotected sex. You could get pregnant or get a venereal disease. You could upset or anger your parents, hurt your reputation or your emotional well-being. But today, in the face of AIDS, if you have unprotected sex, you could pay with your life. It's estimated that as many as 20% of all people living with AIDS today could have been infected as teenagers.

Ben: *"I don't look down on people who don't have sex. Sometimes I think they are smarter because they realize they aren't ready or they don't want to and they have the guts and the character and the presence of mind to say no and to wait. I respect that."*

DECIDING ABOUT SEX

If you decide you want to have sex, it would be a good idea to ask yourself some questions first. Is anyone pressuring you to have sex? Are you afraid *not* to have sex? Do you want to have sex because it's the thing to do? How will you feel about this decision a few months down the road, say, if you are no longer seeing the guy or girl? What does the voice inside you tell you to do? Think it through, and remember that you will have to live with the consequences of your decision. Make the decision that is best for you. If you do something only because another person is pressuring you, you might make a decision you will regret. Sometimes it takes practice to make good decisions. But try it. You'll like the way it makes you feel.

People have sex for many reasons. Sometimes people have sex to feel more accepted or loved. That can get you into trouble. You may end up feeling worse if that person rejects you. If you are having sex so someone will like you more, that's a clue it might be the wrong time to have

"In this day and age you have to grow up faster and take responsibility at a younger age. Part of the joy of being a child is being care-free. But now, unfortunately, you cannot be completely carefree because one careless incident can be fatal."

—Ali Gertz

sex. Before you decide to have sex, weigh the consequences. Make sure you feel good about your decision.

Remember, there are a lot of ways to share emotional and physical closeness with another person besides sex. But if you decide you want sexual intercourse to be part of your relationship, respect each other enough to be as safe as you can be. Use protection.

IT'S *YOUR* LIFE

Alexei: *"I think the pressure to have sex is more prevalent among guys. Girls aren't asking each other, 'Did you get it, did you get it?' I think guys have to deal with the macho issue so they feel accepted by their friends, so they can talk about it."*

The teenage years can be among the toughest of your life—not many people would argue with that. So many things happen so quickly. This can test your confidence and may be one reason you are so susceptible to peer pressure. Just at the time when you are trying to figure out who you are, others (who are just as confused as you are) are telling you how you should act.

It's normal to want to be liked and accepted. But it's impossible to make everyone happy. What's important is to surround yourself with friends who respect and accept you the way you are, so when it comes time to make an important decision, like where to go to college or whether or not to have sex, you're more likely to do what's right for *you.*

Chapter Six

DRUGS & THE RISK OF AIDS

I t seems that every time we flip the dial on the television or radio, we are bombarded with warnings about drugs. We are urged to "Just Say No." Even if you think the message is simplistic, rejecting drugs makes sense. There are reports each year of overdoses and fatal reactions to drugs. Every day, drugs, including alcohol, play a role in automobile accidents that kill innocent people.

Drugs can ease inhibitions, making it easier for people to talk, laugh, and socialize. But they can also cause you to do and say things you regret. If you have tried drugs and liked their effect, it might be hard for you to believe they can be deadly. Maybe you think you can use drugs and not get hurt, or quit anytime. But if you share needles to inject drugs— just once—you could be shooting the AIDS virus into your arm. And if you are high on drugs, you might be more apt to throw caution to the wind and have sex without protection.

Aaron: *"Anyone who decides to do drugs is not playing with a full deck. People who are high do things they normally wouldn't do if they were straight. Drugs mess up your body and your mind, which affects how you relate to people and what choices you make."*

ONE SURE WAY TO PUT YOURSELF AT RISK

Drugs (cocaine, speed, heroin, and other narcotics) sometimes are injected into the vein with a needle and syringe. This is called "mainlining." When drugs are injected just under the skin to be absorbed into the body, it's called "skin-popping."

When a person prepares to shoot drugs, he sticks the needle into a vein and pulls back on the plunger to see whether blood fills the syringe, making sure the needle is in the vein and that he "has a hit." If the drug user has a hit, the drug isn't "wasted" by missing the vein.

More blood enters the syringe when a drug user "boots" the drug. This is when someone injects the drug, then pulls blood back into the syringe, and reinjects it two or three times. Some drug users claim this gives them extra hits of the drug's effect. Others say it's to make sure they have used all the drug particles in the syringe.

Regardless of why someone does it, using a bloody syringe is a sure way of getting infected with the AIDS virus. If you use a needle and syringe without properly cleaning it with bleach, you are risking infection. Even a tiny amount of the AIDS virus, injected directly into the

Alexei: *I definitely want to be the best I can be. Like with swimming, I've been doing it for a long time, and I'm strong and I'm good at it, and I really feel good when I'm doing it. I feel proud that I've worked hard to develop myself in swimming. There's nothing that feels as good as achieving something you've aimed for.*

bloodstream, can be enough to infect another person.

The paraphernalia, or "works," used by drug users can also be contaminated with the AIDS virus. People may use a bottle cap or a spoon to hold the drug while they are shooting up. This is called "the cooker." A piece of cotton or a cigarette filter is often used to separate impurities from the drug. Both the cooker and the cotton can be contaminated with blood containing HIV as the drug is taken in and out of the syringe. Anyone who uses contaminated paraphernalia for shooting up may become infected.

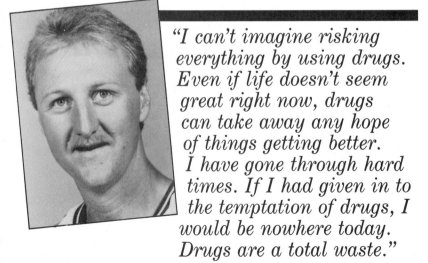

"I can't imagine risking everything by using drugs. Even if life doesn't seem great right now, drugs can take away any hope of things getting better. I have gone through hard times. If I had given in to the temptation of drugs, I would be nowhere today. Drugs are a total waste."

—Larry Bird, *Professional basketball player*

"I NEVER FELT LIKE I FIT IN"

Alison, 36
Has AIDS

Alison looks carefree, doesn't she? If you met her you would be charmed by her sense of humor and her seemingly endless energy. But years ago, Alison stuck a needle contaminated with the AIDS virus into her arm. Now she has AIDS. Alison tries to explain to her 6-year-old son and her 11-year-old daughter that she is sick and may die, though it is difficult for the children to understand that their mother might leave them.

As a teenager, Alison felt insecure. She wanted everyone's approval. She thought that if she got high with other kids, they would like her more. And she liked the effects of drugs. They dulled her feelings. Before Alison knew what was happening, she got hooked. Her life became a nightmare.

Take a few minutes to read the memories she jotted down on a recent hot summer afternoon. You may remember her story for a long time.

"I am lying on the warm beach and I throw my head to the sun, close my eyes, and try to make sense of my life. Memories

PJ: *"Drugs slow down your body and your mind. Eventually, you will get to a point where you can't concentrate on what you really want to do. You lose all sense of responsibility."*

start flooding back to me. I see myself as a painfully shy, lonely, and insecure 14-year-old girl. I used to come to this beach and sit up on the seawall and drink beer. How could I have known where a can of beer or the seemingly innocent days and nights on the beach smoking pot would lead? How could I know? My parents never talked about those issues. In fact, things appeared very normal in my home. I lived in a perfect little white Cape Cod–style home with aquamarine shutters. The fence around the house was covered with roses. I looked like the typical suburban kid with long blonde hair and the best sweaters and shoes. I needed a lot of material things to camouflage the way I felt inside. I had always been extremely lonely and never felt like I fit in. I had a lot of fear of just living.

"In school, there were two groups of people: the squares, or bookworms, and the cheerleaders. I was smart, but the honor students bored me. I was too shy to be a cheerleader. I found my people in the kids with long hair, torn jeans, and silver jewelry. It all said 'freedom.' My parents freaked. But the more they freaked, the more radical I got. Pressure from my parents never mattered much to me. What mattered to me was being accepted by my friends. They defined my lifestyle. And that meant a lot of drugs.

"It just seemed natural to smoke the joint when it was handed to me, to drop my first tab of acid when it was offered, and to sniff glue. It seemed so innocent. Even though I wanted to be high all the time, I didn't believe I could get addicted. I thought I could stop at any time. I wasn't like the junkies in New York. After all, I was a suburban kid just out for a good time. And I liked it. I won't lie. I was able to take drugs and then laugh and talk and be myself.

"But addiction is a very insidious thing. You never know if you will become addicted when you pick up that first joint. I chose to risk it because I thought I was invincible. I never imagined I would end up in the gutter, homeless, jobless, my life broken apart and strewn about like pieces of trash blowing over some inner-city slum. Not me, the perfect little child from Beverly, Massachusetts. I wouldn't listen to anyone who told me to stop taking drugs and drinking. No way. I told them I knew what I was doing, thank you very much. I kept getting deeper into drugs and was actually unaware it was all happening.

"One day when I was 16, I was with a few of my older friends. We were in a car and some guy I had a crush on was shooting heroin. I mean this dude was cool. He was a drummer in a band. His hair was to his shoulders. When he handed me his needle and syringe, I got a rush of energy that told me it was forbidden but exciting. I didn't shoot heroin for a couple more months. When I did, someone had to fix it for me and shoot it into my arm, and I used someone else's needle. I didn't get hooked right away. But I had the first taste of what would become my drug of choice.

"Who would ever dream by looking at my picture in the school yearbook that I would turn into a dope fiend? It didn't happen overnight. It was a long, slow process. My addiction seemed to creep into every area of my life until finally I was so submerged in it, nothing else mattered to me. I used drugs for years.

"At the age of 24 I had a baby and got an apartment. I tried to be a normal mother. It didn't work. My home was overrun with junkies. I just couldn't stay straight. I had another baby. I started stealing. Finally, I was busted and taken away to the women's prison in chains and handcuffs. Twenty-two hours a day for a week I was locked in a chilly cell, shaking from the cold and from withdrawal from drugs. My children had been taken away from me and the relationship I had with a guy ended. I was a mess. I had plenty of time to think. I realized I couldn't go on. I couldn't pay the price any longer.

Ben: *One of the hardest things to handle would be the inevitability of death. There are so many things I want to do in my life. I want to be given the chance to become someone. I want to see how the story ends. I don't want to die.*

"Five days after I got out of prison, with sunken cheeks, tangled hair, and blood-stained jeans, I entered drug treatment. Somewhere between that day and two years of intense treatment I made my way back to society. I started working with addicts and decided to go to college, where I remained on the dean's list for three semesters. The sun was shining at last. I was free of dope.

"After my third year of drug recovery, I found myself completely exhausted. I had been back and forth to the doctor for sinus infections and a case of thrush. One doctor suggested I get tested for the AIDS virus. I became defensive and indignant. I wrote all my symptoms off to stress. Like who wouldn't be stressed, right? Full-time college, two kids, working in a drug recovery program. Finally I broke out in a rash called shingles. By then, most of the people I had shot dope with were either dead or had tested positive. After lengthy talks with a friend, I agreed to be tested. In my gut I knew the results before the nurse even opened the envelope. I tested positive. I froze, went numb, and remained that way for about a week. I just didn't feel anything. I just sat there wondering how God could be so unfair. Hadn't I paid enough? My rage was incredible and directed mainly at God. Hadn't I prayed hard enough or asked for

Alexei: *I want to see the world. I want to see how other people live. I want to explore and see all the things that are out there.*

enough help or shown enough gratitude? I hated this disease of addiction. It just wouldn't let me forget who I had been or where I had come from. I hated life and wanted to die—just to get it over with quick. I would say things like, 'I got straight just for this?' I thought of shooting dope, but that didn't even fit into my life. Somewhere, in a sane moment, I decided that if I was going to die, it was going to be with some dignity. At least my babies could say I was a *recovering* addict.

"I made it into the fall semester of college that year, and my grades remained good but the workload was killing me. By January break I couldn't move off the couch, I couldn't eat—I just lay there frustrated and in pain. One evening in March I collapsed. Fever racked my body. I ached all over and knew this was it, I was going to die. I had been diagnosed as having a severe kidney infection. I never felt so weak and powerless in all my life. I hated feeling so helpless, so out of control, so I tried to get up to do something for myself. I tried to wash the dishes but had to be helped back to bed by my 11-year-old daughter. These kids had seen so much but still didn't realize what was happening to me. We sat in my bed that night and I explained that I might die. Maybe God wanted Mommy with Him, I told my daughter. I explained that I was very sick and had caught a virus when I was on the street shooting dope. I reassured her that heaven was a nice place with lots of light, that God and I would always be looking down on her and Josh, and that I loved her and her brother very much.

"In the following days I slowly regained my strength. The angry injustice I once felt has been replaced with quiet contentment, and I realize I am a lot happier now than any day I was high on dope. Although AIDS is part of my life, today it doesn't own me. I try to put things in God's hands and have come to the conclusion that He didn't take me out of 18 years of hellish addiction to die—not just yet. I still have lots of work to do on earth. I am reasonably sane, happy, and at peace, living with AIDS."

If you know people who have used drugs, you may have felt pressure, like Alison did, to try them. And you, too, might be tempted to try drugs to block out bad feelings. But those feelings of inadequacy, rejection, and insecurity are a part of life. Give yourself a chance to feel the ups and downs of life. That's how people develop emotionally. Drugs will surely make it hard—if not impossible—for you to achieve your potential.

"I THOUGHT DRUGS WOULD MAKE ME FEEL BETTER"

Robert, 33
Has AIDS

Tanya: *"AIDS doesn't just happen to older people – but to all people who put themselves at risk."*

Robert grew up in a home filled with music. His mother and father loved jazz and the blues. His sister played the African drums. His brother loved Spanish music. Robert, the youngest, enjoyed it all.

"I loved the clarinet and the keyboard. Music made me feel good."

As a teenager, Robert would sit on the front steps of his house and make up songs on his clarinet. He dreamed of traveling and performing all over the world. At 16, Robert got sidetracked.

"I started drugs out of curiosity and stupidity. I didn't think drugs would do what they did to me. I was always told to stay away from drugs, that they would mess me up. But I thought I could handle them. I thought I was bigger than drugs."

Before long Robert was spending more time shooting heroin than playing his music. Drugs proved more powerful than Robert—he was addicted. He started living the life of an addict. That meant breaking into neighbors' houses and stealing whatever he could sell.

"I thought drugs would make me feel better. They made me miserable. I woke up depressed every morning."

Robert tried to give up drugs dozens of times. It never worked. The lure of the drug was too strong. Finally, after 13 years of running from police, Robert entered a drug treatment program. He had seen too many friends die. He wanted to go straight—and he did with the help of the program. He found a new, better life. Money he earned from a job as a construction worker was spent on clothes, food, and rent instead of on drugs. He got himself back in good physical condition. He dated. Life was good.

Five years later, Robert got a cold that he couldn't shake. It hung on for weeks. Purple marks appeared on his arm. On a friend's advice, he got tested for HIV. The test came back positive. The purple spots were Kaposi's sarcoma, an AIDS-related cancer.

"Even though I have been clean for over five years, I have found out AIDS is going to kill me. I used drugs without caring about the consequences. I have a lot of broken dreams. I am not messing with drugs now, but it's too late for me."

Robert doesn't know when he got infected—it could have been as many as 10

Aaron: *"The worst part of having AIDS would be that there is no specific timetable. You could get sick and die within 6 months, or it could go on for 5 or 10 years. You can't be cured and you don't know when it is going to kill you."*

years ago. He worries that he may have passed the AIDS virus on to some of his sex partners. He worries that someone will die just because she had sex with him.

The guilt weighs heavily on Robert. If he could, he would turn back the clock and make different choices. He says teenagers today have that opportunity.

"I thought I could just do drugs once or twice. There is no once or twice, especially if you get what you think are good results. After a while, drugs are not going to make you feel better, just more miserable.

"Pay attention to someone you trust . . . your parents, a teacher, a neighbor. If you don't have a good role model, get one. Life is a one-shot deal; the contract is for one shot. Don't throw it away."

STRAIGHT TALK FROM A TEACHER

Larry Aaronson,
High school teacher,
Cambridge,
Massachusetts

"**K**ids come to me to talk about drugs. Some tell me they are tempted to try them or already have. Others are worried about friends who are messing with drugs. I guess they come to me because they know they can trust me. They know I will talk straight about the risks and the realities without judging them. Don't get me wrong, I don't make it any secret around the school how I feel about drugs. The students know I am not permissive. But they know I care. I am there as a sounding board and I will try to help if I think a kid is headed for trouble.

Barbara: *"You wouldn't be able to think about your future—it would be bleak."*

"There are trustworthy adults kids can talk to—the real issue is finding them. Usually you don't have to look very hard. Some kids have told me they didn't have anyone in their lives they could trust enough to talk to. I really push that point. Frankly, when someone says that, I am afraid it's just an excuse to keep isolating themselves and to keep using drugs because I don't know anyone who has *no one* to talk to. There are adults who are deeply committed to helping kids and who can be trusted—people who have made it their business to help. Sometimes the best way to find out who they are is to ask around.

"Some kids can't talk with their parents—there is no question about it. But one thing I have seen over and over again is kids misjudging their parents. So often parents are willing to talk openly and listen and help. Most parents do love their kids and want to be there for them. Many parents went through similar conflicting times as teenagers. But if a kid can't talk to his or her parents, I say, 'Don't give up. Reach out, because it will make all the difference in the world.' "

It's true—if you talk to adults you trust or respect about pressures you feel, you might learn that they once felt the same way. If you can get some perspective from an older person who has been through a tough time and survived, it might help you hang in there and keep trying until life seems a little easier.

There is not a teenager alive who doesn't struggle with his or her self-worth at one time or another. And there's not an adult who doesn't remember the agony of the teenage years.

Drugs may temporarily ease feelings of pressure or inadequacy. But think about it: The "high" from a drug doesn't last forever. And it doesn't take away the bad feelings. It just covers them up. When the drug wears off, the bad feelings are still there, sometimes even worse. When you are feeling really lousy about yourself, it helps to talk to someone you trust. It might not solve your problem, but just getting it off your chest can help you feel better and it might give you some perspective. Sometimes that can make all the difference in the world.

Everyone knows drugs and alcohol af-

Alexei: *"It's tough because you are going through a lot of changes in your life. You are experimenting with many new things. I am asking myself, should I do this? Or is this good for me? Should I join this club, or should I have sex, or should I drink? It's really hard to know which way to go. That's when you have to go inside yourself and really find out what you want to do and what feels comfortable. So it's really hard being a teenager in those ways."*

"*I think it is pretty well documented—and a fact that I take pride in—that I do not smoke, drink, or do drugs. This was a decision I made a long time ago, even though I had to deal with peer pressure —everyone does. But when I realized that the only person I truly had to impress was myself, I decided to work hard at my craft and do what it took to be a success. Well, I have worked hard and have achieved a lot because I stuck to the promise I made to myself. You, too, can make the decision to do what's right—stay away from things that will mess you up, stay in school and work hard. Make that promise to yourself and reach for the sky.*"

—Eddie Murphy, *Actor*

fect a person's ability to think clearly and make good decisions. If you are high, you may be more apt to have sex without protection. You might not stop to think about it, or you may tell yourself you have nothing to be concerned about. That is dangerous.

"COCAINE BECAME MY LIFE"

Barbara: *"I guess there have been times I have felt kind of lonely. For example, when I am home on a Friday night and I call my friends and find out they are out with other people I'm not friends with. That's something that's been hard for me. It's not like I have a hard time fitting in, but I guess I am just very aware there are special groups. I don't really want to be a part of any one group, but sometimes I feel lonely."*

Phil, a former cocaine addict, recalls his nightmare. "Cocaine can make you want to have a lot of sex. I got to a point where I would do anything for that experience. If I couldn't find my girlfriend I would start scrambling. The fantasy (and that is what it was, a fantasy) was so strong that I would go with anyone . . . and believe me, protecting myself during sex wasn't even in my mind. I never thought about that. And 90% of the time, it didn't work out the way I wanted it to anyway, you know what I mean? But I kept chasing the experience, to the exclusion of everything else in my life . . . my job, my family, my health, my friends. Cocaine became my life. Cocaine leads you around by the nose, the arm, the lungs. You want to play with fire, live on the edge? I say find something else. Cocaine shouldn't even be considered a choice. You have to decide how much your life is worth . . . and whether your whole life is worth risking for cocaine."

Crack is a highly addictive form of cocaine that is smoked, not injected or snorted. Some addicts insist they became addicted the *first time* they smoked crack. The addiction is so powerful, they say they would do anything to get the drug, including selling sex. If you are craving a drug, the last thing on your mind is safer sex or, as the following story about Jashine will show, avoiding other destructive behavior.

"FROM THAT FIRST TRY, YOU CAN DIE"

Although pregnant and just days away from having a baby, Jashine looks small and fragile. Her soft brown hair is pulled back in a braid. Her brown eyes dart around the playground following her 1½-year-old son. Jashine talks non-stop. She says if she is quiet, she starts to think and cries. You see, the same day Jashine and her husband celebrated the

Jashine, 22
Infected
with the
AIDS virus

news that she was pregnant with their second child, her nurse gave her devastating news.

"She told me I was HIV-positive, infected with the AIDS virus. I laughed. I told her I didn't believe her; I told her to do it again. So she did. It came back positive again. That time I cried. I felt scared, lonely, confused, and tired."

How Jashine became infected is no mystery. As a teenager, she used drugs to smother the pain of the abuse she had suffered as a child. A marijuana habit turned into an addiction to crack. Today, Jashine is drug-free. But one night, high on crack, she made a mistake—a deadly one.

"I was getting high with some girls I know. They were IV-drug users. I was so up on the cocaine, I needed something to bring me down, so I let one of the girls stick a needle in my arm. Now I've got AIDS."

Jashine knows she will be infected forever. She prays every day that her baby isn't born infected. And she prays she doesn't die before her children are grown.

"I worry about my baby dying, that I might have her a month or two and then she might die. And I wonder, what will happen to my kids if I die? Will they be raised right? Will my husband be with another woman? If so, will she take care of them properly? I want to be around when

PJ: *"There are a lot of pressures. Sometimes you have to worry about what other people think or say, but I don't base my life on it. Making decisions is the hardest part, asking yourself, 'Am I doing what's right?'"*

my son goes to school. I want to be with him when he needs me, and I know now it might not be possible."

That one act, sticking a needle in her arm that *one time*, has devastated Jashine and her family.

"Don't do drugs if you have never done them. You don't need to be like one of the crowd. And who knows, from that first try, you can die. If you are going to have sex, even if you've known a person for a while, you can't just say, 'Let me see your blood test.' Take precautions if you have sex: Use condoms. If the person doesn't want to or says, 'That is no good; I can't feel it,' then don't have sex."

A RUNAWAY'S STORY

Deborah, 24
Infected with the
AIDS virus
Steven, 7
Amber, 4
Aaron, 9 months

Growing up, Deborah had nine stepmothers. Can you imagine how confused she must have felt? When she was only three, her mother deserted the family. Her relationship with her father was always strained.

"When I turned 14, I became interested in boys. I wanted to date and go out with friends, but my father wouldn't let me. My stepmother at the time was an alcoholic.

Ben: *"What's hard about being a teen is, I guess, caring so much about what people think of you. That's human nature. If someone didn't care what people thought, he would probably become a hermit. Everyone, to a certain extent, wants to fit in or impress someone or do something that has an effect on another person. But if you are thinking about that all the time, you can put a lot of pressure on yourself."*

She worked in a pizza parlor and when she got done with work, she'd sit there at the pizza parlor and drink till it was time to come home. Then she and my father would get into a fight. She'd come in and start pushing me around. Finally, I had enough and I ran away."

Deborah supported herself working as a waitress in a roadside restaurant. The salary was low and tips weren't great, so she slept at the Salvation Army shelter and got hot meals at a soup kitchen. When she was 17 she met an outgoing, handsome guy. Deborah became pregnant and they got married. They had a second child. She thought her life was straightening out.

"After a while, I found out he was shooting drugs to get high. I tried it a few times, but I felt guilty. You can't be a good mother while you are high on drugs. We both quit."

Soon after they got straight, Deborah found out she was pregnant again. Everyone was talking about AIDS, and she worried she might be infected and pass the virus on to her baby. So she got tested. Her worst fears were realized—Deborah had been infected with HIV.

"I sat down and cried and cried and cried. It's scary. I didn't think it could happen to me. I thought I was just going to get high a couple of times—but it ruined my life."

Tests on Deborah's baby show he is probably not infected with the AIDS virus, though it's too early to be sure. Deborah says her husband is infected, too. (She doesn't know if she contracted the virus from him or by sharing a needle with another drug user.) She is terrified that her children will grow up without a mother, just as she did.

"I see the love and friendship between mothers and their children on television and I say, 'Hey, I never had that.' I needed my mom, and she wasn't there. Now I wonder, am I going to be at Amber's wedding? Am I going to see my grandchildren? My kids are going to be alone. They aren't going to have a mommy and daddy. It's not their fault. It's our fault. That's the only thing I worry about: What will happen to my kids when we are gone? I want to live. I have three beautiful reasons to live."

The death of a parent is emotionally devastating for a child. In the next decade, the AIDS epidemic will claim thousands of mothers and fathers. The New York Department of Public Health estimates that by the year 1995, more than 20,000 children in that city will become orphans because of AIDS. Experts worry that there will not be enough people willing to care for these children.

Aaron: *"I resent the lack of respect from adults. I want so badly to be taken seriously—and so often I feel adults don't respect teenagers.*

HALE HOUSE, FOR CHILDREN

Many children who lose one or both parents to AIDS are shuttled from one relative to another. Brothers and sisters are often separated. Imagine what it would be like for a child who is grieving the loss of his mother or father to suddenly lose his sense of family, his friends, and his schoolmates as well.

For more than twenty years, children in New York City, abandoned by drug-addicted and alcoholic parents, have found a temporary home at Hale House. Dr. Lorraine Hale and her mother, Clara Hale, have loved and cared for more than eight hundred children before finding them loving homes.

Now Hale House is caring for children abandoned and orphaned by parents with AIDS. Some of these babies have also tested positive for the AIDS virus. Finding these children homes can be difficult for a number of reasons. Fear is one factor; people who aren't educated about how the AIDS virus is transmitted worry that they could become infected simply by caring for a child with AIDS. And others worry about becoming attached to a child who has a fatal disease. It takes especially loving and patient men and women to make homes for these youngsters. So the challenge Hale House now faces in finding homes for these children is greater than ever.

"When one of our children is considered 'cute,' that youngster stands a chance of being adopted. However, one who doesn't fit the popular conception of 'cute' might not be selected.

"We have a three-year-old whose father is dying of AIDS. Her mother has AIDS. Also, according to the norm, she would not be considered a pretty child. She is moody and difficult. We are concerned that no one will want to take her. In the meantime, we give her a lot of affection and attention, but she needs her own family. We shall have to work a little harder to find a family for this little girl. But we are very determined."

—Dr. Lorraine Hale, *Hale House*

Chapter Seven

A BAD WAY TO DIE

Teenagers might have a tendency to ignore warnings about the dangers of sharing needles and having unprotected sex. As one 16-year-old girl said, "I'm going to die from something; it might as well be AIDS." If you believe that, then you probably have never met anyone with AIDS. Death from AIDS is often disfiguring, painful, and slow. When someone shares needles or has sex without protection, they are risking that fate.

Eddie, 30
Died of AIDS

THE HORROR OF AIDS

Eddie wanted people to know the horror of AIDS. He allowed a series of photographs of himself to be taken over the course of his illness so others could look at them and better understand the disease.

Before he got sick, when Eddie walked into a room, chances are you'd notice him. If you didn't, and he wanted your attention, he would talk loudly or crack a joke.

"I have always been a dramatic person, always a person who likes to be the center of attention," Eddie once said.

Even as a youngster, Eddie loved to perform. He was three when his father, who is Armenian, taught Eddie the Armenian belly dance. Eddie perfected the cultural folk dance and performed in local clubs and on television.

"I loved being in front of the camera. My form of entertainment was very unusual. Most people think, 'Oh, you're a belly dancer, you're a go-go dancer.' That's not what I did. I was fully dressed all the time and we had seven musicians behind us. It was something I did since I was a little boy, dancing to Middle Eastern music because that's the first music I heard."

But Eddie couldn't make a steady living performing, so he took a job with an airline as a reservations agent.

Eddie had an extraordinary ability to handle people. He could make angry customers laugh or tense customers relax. People felt good talking to Eddie.

But in his personal life, Eddie was a

worrier. He worried about what people thought of him, whether they could see through his insecurities. He worried about his mother and father growing older and getting sick. And he worried about his own health. Lately, he had been feeling tired. The week before his 28th birthday, he went to the doctor for an exam.

"I went to the health clinic and was given a physical. He was feeling around the lymph nodes in my neck and he went, 'Hmmmm,' you know, and I said, 'Oh-oh.' He said, 'There is a little, ah, well you probably won't even feel it.' I put my finger on it and said, 'No, I don't feel it.' "

The doctor told Eddie to keep an eye on the swollen lymph node and let him know if it grew.

But Eddie went to another doctor who told him the lump should be removed. "He said, 'It's probably benign, but let's take it out.' And I thought, 'My God, they are using cancer words.' "

The lump was not cancerous. But the doctor knew something was wrong. He

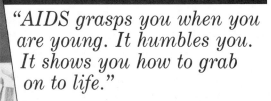

"AIDS grasps you when you are young. It humbles you. It shows you how to grab on to life."

"Some days I say I don't want anyone to love me anymore because they are going to be so hurt. I do feel bad about that."

said, "I want to do a blood test." Eddie agreed, saying, "You know, I am a gay man. You might want to test for the AIDS virus." His doctor drew a sample of blood.

Eddie knew people with AIDS. In the past, he had had unprotected sex. He was prepared for bad news. A week or so later Eddie got the results, which showed he had been exposed to the AIDS virus. "When the doctor told me, I wasn't shocked. I didn't ask, 'Why me?'"

Eddie worked for several months and tried to keep his mind occupied. He obsessed about his health. He knew his AIDS was torture for his mother and father. He remembered their response when, at 16, he told them he was gay: "You are our son, Eddie. We love you no matter what."

One day, driving home from work, it all caught up with him. He sped down the highway with tears streaming down his face. "I was tired and just sobbing. I was thinking, 'What a mess you have gotten yourself into.' It was one of those times I could actually see how AIDS has really devastated my life, my family's life, my really close friends. I was pretty angry and sad."

As months passed, Eddie was ravaged by cancer. A lot of his energy was spent helping his mother and father cope with the nightmare of watching their son die.

"My father puts on a front because he thinks he is supposed to. He thinks that's how men should act, though at times he cries and says, 'No, you can't go!' I didn't know that I would ultimately hurt them. And they would never blame me. That is how good they are."

Eddie died 19 months after his diagnosis. He had always wanted to be famous. "Devastatingly famous is what I wanted to be. It took me a long time to get over the fact that I wasn't going to be a household name."

Those who knew Eddie say his desire to share his story shows his concern for others. Eddie acknowledged: "Yeah, I can probably make a little bit of a difference."

"I was careful. I used to use condoms. But obviously there were times I didn't use them."

Jack Armitage, Eddie's friend

Jack Armitage and Eddie were friends for years before Eddie got sick with AIDS. Jack is the executive director of Strongest Link, an organization in Topsfield, Massachusetts, that cares for people infected with HIV.

Toward the end of Eddie's illness, Jack became Eddie's arms and legs, carrying him to the bathroom, bathing him, and trying to keep Eddie comfortable. Often that meant massaging his thin, weak body.

"Eddie had one of the symptoms of AIDS called 'night sweats.' Sweat is one of the body fluids that doesn't transmit the AIDS virus. So, even if my hands were touching him, I wouldn't have any hesitation about taking care of him."

Jack has had close contact with many people with AIDS. He says if people *could* become infected through close, casual contact, surely he and a lot of other people would be infected by now.

Chapter Eight
QUESTIONS

Barbara: *"Even if you feel intimate with a person, you don't know his sexual history. It's always important to be more cautious than not. Also, condoms can prevent other things such as pregnancy and sexually transmitted diseases. If you don't use condoms . . . you may very well regret it."*

You probably have many questions about how someone can become infected with the AIDS virus. Even if a question seems goofy, it's worth asking because good answers to all your questions about AIDS will help you become more comfortable with the facts. And you will begin to understand that *you* control whether you get infected or not. The following are the questions most frequently asked about the transmission of the AIDS virus:

Can I get infected with HIV, the AIDS virus, by sitting next to someone who is infected?

No. In all the years the AIDS virus has been around, no one has ever been infected that way. Of the thousands of doctors and nurses who have cared for people with AIDS, none has ever become infected by simply touching or being with someone who was infected with the virus. Also, researchers have studied thousands of mothers and fathers, sisters and brothers, and friends of people with AIDS.

Often family members share toothbrushes and bathrooms and eat off the same dishes.

Can I get infected with the AIDS virus from a mosquito?

No. For the mosquito to be able to infect a person, it would have to reproduce the virus. Researchers know mosquitoes can't do that.

Can I get infected with the AIDS virus if someone with AIDS sneezes on me?

No. HIV, the AIDS virus, does not live in mucus in your nose. It's just not there. And experts agree that any virus that may be present in the saliva would not be enough to cause infection.

Can I get infected with the AIDS virus in a swimming pool?

No. For you to get infected, HIV must get into your bloodstream through blood, semen, or vaginal fluids. If any of these fluids were floating around in a swimming pool, any virus in them would be killed quickly by chlorine.

Can I get infected with the AIDS virus by sitting on a toilet seat?

No. The AIDS virus is fragile. It cannot

live outside of the body. Any HIV in blood or urine on a toilet seat would die quickly. Remember this: The AIDS virus can't pass through unbroken skin. To infect a person, the AIDS virus must enter the bloodstream.

Can I get infected with the AIDS virus even if I am on the birth control pill?

Yes. Some people make the mistake of believing the Pill works by killing sperm. That is *not* how the Pill works. The Pill contains the synthetic hormones estrogen and progesterone, which suppress the natural hormone cycle. This prevents the release of the egg. If the female doesn't release the egg, there is no chance of pregnancy. The Pill doesn't kill sperm, nor does it kill the AIDS virus. Neither the diaphragm nor the IUD will protect you against the AIDS virus either, for the same reason.

Can I get infected by deep kissing, or French kissing, someone who is infected with the AIDS virus?

Researchers aren't 100% sure. But there are no reported cases of AIDS from kissing. Researchers have examined the saliva of people infected with the AIDS virus and found tiny amounts of the virus in some of the samples. Experts agree that the small amount of virus present in those people's saliva would not be enough to spread infection. Infection might occur if an infected person with a bleeding cut in the mouth were kissing another person who also had a cut on the gums or the inside of the cheek. If blood infected with HIV is passed to another person, there is always the chance of infection. This means that if you don't have open bleeding cuts or sores in your mouth, you can probably enjoy kissing without worrying about AIDS.

PJ: *"I would be afraid I might lose all contact with my friends because they would be afraid they could get the virus from me."*

Can I get infected with the AIDS virus by shaking hands with someone infected with the AIDS virus?

No. The virus has to get into your blood; it cannot pass through intact skin. If a person with a large, open sore on his hand shook hands with a person infected with the virus who also had a bloody sore on his hand, there would be a slight chance of infection. But what is the likelihood of two people with oozing, bloody sores shaking hands?

Remember, people who are infected with HIV, the AIDS virus, can sometimes feel lonely and frightened. They need physical contact, love, and compassion.

Can I get infected with the AIDS virus by touching a doorknob?

No. As you've already read, the AIDS virus needs a direct route to your bloodstream. Is there blood, semen, or vaginal fluids on the doorknob? Do you have an open sore on your hand? Don't forget, the AIDS virus is fragile. It dies when it comes into contact with air. And it cannot pass through unbroken skin.

Can I get infected with the AIDS virus by using a public telephone?

No. Even if someone coughs on the telephone, the AIDS virus exists in such tiny amounts in the saliva of some infected people, that there couldn't possibly be enough on the telephone to infect anyone. But more important, the AIDS virus dies when it comes in contact with air.

Can I get infected with the AIDS virus by sharing eye makeup?

No. Like saliva, there is very little or no AIDS virus in tears. The small amount that could be present would die quickly if exposed to air. But there are a lot of other germs in your eyes. If you do use someone else's mascara or eyeliner, you could get an eye infection. So it's best not to share eye makeup *anyway*.

Can I get infected with the AIDS virus by touching another person's sweat?

No. Researchers have not found the AIDS virus in sweat.

Can I get infected with the AIDS virus through oral sex?

Yes, a few cases have been reported. Though no one is sure how much risk is involved in oral sex, there are ways of reducing your risk. If you are having oral sex with a woman, make sure she is not menstruating, since the AIDS virus could

"Our experience has been that young people have a desire to help those less fortunate. One easy way for you to help save a life is to donate blood. It is important for healthy people who are not at risk for AIDS to become donors so there will be blood on hand when it is needed. You can't get AIDS from giving blood."

—Dr. Lewllys Barker,
Former Chief Medical Officer, American Red Cross

be in her menstrual blood. If you are having oral sex with a man, remember, the AIDS virus can be in semen and pre-ejaculation fluids. A condom should be used for protection when engaging in oral sex with a man. He should *not* ejaculate in your mouth.

Can I become infected with the AIDS virus by eating food from an infected person's plate?

No. Studies done with families of people with AIDS show that HIV is not transmitted by sharing food and utensils with a person with AIDS. The AIDS virus cannot live outside of the body.

Can I get infected with the AIDS virus by donating blood?

No. You cannot get infected by donating blood. When you give blood, the blood is going out of your body and into a bag. Blood is not going into your body and you are not exposed to anyone else's blood. The needle used to draw your blood is always new and sterile. Then it's destroyed and cannot be used again for any purpose.

If I think I haven't been exposed to the AIDS virus, can I donate blood?

Yes. If you are *certain* you haven't been

exposed to the AIDS virus you *should* donate blood—people need it! But if there's any chance at all that you have been exposed, don't do it. Although blood banks test all the blood that is donated, if you were exposed in the last six months or so, you may not yet have developed antibodies to HIV in your blood, in which case your blood would *seem* safe to add to the blood supply. Before donating blood, read all the written material you are given and answer questions honestly. People who need blood rely on *you* to be honest.

If I have been having sex with more than one partner and haven't been using condoms, should I start using them now?

Yes. Your chances of infection with the AIDS virus go up with the number of sex partners you have and with the frequency of sexual activity. There is no way of predicting whether you would be infected by your first exposure or your 100th exposure to the AIDS virus. And if you may have been infected, use condoms starting now so you don't pass the virus on. Condoms are not a 100% guarantee against infection with HIV, the AIDS virus, or other sexually transmitted diseases, so to protect your physical health and your emotional well-being, it's a good idea to limit the number of sex partners you have.

Chapter Nine

VACCINES AND TREATMENTS

Through the years, scientists have successfully developed vaccines for many infectious diseases, including polio, smallpox, measles, mumps, and the flu. Today, around the world many leading researchers are working to develop a vaccine against AIDS. But some experts fear it may be a long time before they are able to do that, if ever—which is why prevention through education is so important.

A vaccine is a shot or a pill that will help protect the body against a certain disease. A vaccine is made with an inactive or killed form of the virus that causes a disease. Sometimes just a piece of the virus, rather than the whole virus, is used. When this killed virus is given to a person, it acts as an antigen or a foreign invader. The body recognizes it as an intruder and mounts an attack by creating antibodies against it. If the person is later exposed to that same type of virus or bacteria, these antibodies will fight it off.

If scientists could develop a vaccine against AIDS, it could eventually stop the spread of the disease. Developing a vaccine against the AIDS virus is a particularly difficult challenge because the AIDS virus is constantly mutating, or changing. To be effective, a vaccine would have to protect against a variety of types of the AIDS virus. Scientists hope they can find a part of the virus that doesn't change and make a vaccine from that.

Another problem in developing a vaccine is the lack of an animal that develops AIDS after infection with the AIDS virus. This would make it easier for scientists to test potential vaccines. Since that animal has not been found yet, scientists have to rely on human volunteers. But what if the vaccine were flawed and caused the volunteer to develop AIDS? And how do you determine whether a vaccine works? Surely not by purposefully exposing a person to the AIDS virus after vaccination. These are tough questions that cause experts to fear there may never be an effective vaccine against HIV. At the very least, it will take years to develop.

For those already infected, there are some treatments.

Alexei: *"Every day you are thinking, 'My life is over. I can't do any of the things I wanted to do.'"*

AZT

AZT was the first drug to be licensed

Ben: *"You are never going to get any better. It is only going downhill."*

by the U.S. government for the treatment of infection with the AIDS virus. AZT is not a new drug. It was developed to fight cancer but wasn't effective. It turns out that AZT blocks the enzyme that the AIDS virus uses to reproduce itself. Because AZT slows reproduction of the virus, it keeps infected people alive longer. Doctors recommend that people infected with the AIDS virus take AZT even if they don't show symptoms of the disease, providing tests show their immune system is beginning to be weakened.

Unfortunately, AZT affects not only the AIDS virus, but also healthy cells. It can damage a person's bone marrow, causing anemia, and also cause irritation to muscles. Many people cannot take AZT because they cannot tolerate these negative side effects. Recently, scientists have found that the AIDS virus can become resistant to AZT.

ddI

The second anti-AIDS drug to win government approval is ddI. This drug acts in a similar way to block the reproduction of the AIDS virus, but it doesn't have the same negative side effects on the blood as AZT, and may be especially useful in patients who develop resistance to AZT.

Some researchers think AZT and ddI will best be used in rotation.

CD4

CD4 is a protein produced in the body. It sits on the surface of a cell and acts as a doorway through which the AIDS virus passes to infect the cell. In laboratories, scientists have found ways to make massive quantities of CD4. Studies show CD4 can act as a decoy. The virus is tricked and is trapped. Once the virus is trapped, it may not enter and infect a healthy cell.

Though the first study with CD4 showed that it was safe and produced no negative side effects, it is still too soon to tell how important a role CD4 will play in treating infection with HIV.

Aerosolized Pentamidine

Pneumonia due to pneumocystis is a major cause of death due to infection among AIDS patients. Pentamidine is an antibiotic that effectively blocks the germ that causes this deadly pneumonia. Originally, doctors gave this drug to patients in the vein or by shots into the muscle, but many

Alexei: *"It would be awful to be in your sickbed. You are still alive but thinking . . ."*

patients had a bad reaction and became ill. Patients tolerate the drug better if it's given in an aerosol spray. Research has shown that by breathing aerosolized pentamidine, 95% of patients were protected from recurrence of pneumonia over the course of one year. Based on that research, the U.S. government has approved aerosolized pentamidine for people with AIDS. Infected people with T-cell counts that have dropped to a certain level also qualify for the drug.

Aerosolized pentamidine is not 100% effective in preventing pneumocystis pneumonia. And long-term negative effects of the drug on the lungs are not yet known.

Interferon

Not much is known about how the AIDS virus actually assembles itself in the cell. Nor is much known about how the virus leaves the cell after multiplying. Researchers have found that a protein in the body called interferon appears to interfere with the ability of the AIDS virus to be produced in cells. In the laboratory, scientists have reproduced large amounts of this body protein. Interferon has proven most effective in AIDS patients with the cancer called Kaposi's sarcoma. Doctors report that it appears to kill some cancer cells in the Kaposi's sarcoma tumors,

Tanya: *"If I had AIDS, I wouldn't live to see how my friends turned out. And I wouldn't reach any of my goals. I would die before that could happen. And I would worry about how my parents would cope if I got AIDS. That is upsetting to think about."*

thereby reducing their size. Scientists believe it may even have some effect against HIV itself. Researchers are exploring the possibility of combining interferon with other drugs such as AZT for the treatment of patients with Kaposi's sarcoma as well as AIDS patients who don't have this cancer.

Ben:_"Like, 'This is the best I am going to feel the rest of my life?' "_

Because certain combinations of drugs are showing some effectiveness in the treatment of the AIDS virus, many health officials say it is important to know whether you are infected. The earlier you know, the earlier you may be treated, which could mean staying well and living longer.

"Every teenager should look in the mirror and say there is no one cooler than you so make your own decisions. This is your only life. So who should call the shots? Start adding up all the good things about yourself. I bet the list will be long enough to proclaim yourself altogether great!"
—Martin Short, _Actor and comedian_

Chapter Ten
TESTING

Tanya: "*I think that if you've had sex and you're worried that you've been exposed to the AIDS virus you ought to seriously consider getting tested and promise yourself you will act responsibly. It's just the right thing to do.*"

As you think back on some things you have done, you might worry that you have been infected. Before jumping to conclusions, talk about your concerns with a teacher or a parent or another adult you trust, or call an AIDS hotline. Someone who knows about AIDS can help you determine whether your concerns are based on myth or fact, and whether you should consider being tested. Many experts agree that it's good to find out early if you are infected with the AIDS virus so you can get appropriate medical care and possibly start taking medications that will keep you healthy longer. Also, if you are infected, you should take steps to make sure you don't spread the virus.

Blood tests are used to determine whether you have been exposed to the AIDS virus. The most commonly used test is called an ELISA (enzyme-linked immunosorbent assay) test. When your body is exposed to a germ or a virus, like the AIDS virus, the immune system mounts an attack against it and makes antibodies (the molecules that help fend off the foreign invader) for that specific germ. The

ELISA test for the AIDS virus tests your blood to determine whether your body has made antibodies to HIV, the AIDS virus, which it will usually do within several months of being infected. If the ELISA test is positive, another test, called the Western Blot test, is performed on the same blood sample to confirm the ELISA test. This is done because occasionally the ELISA test falsely indicates the presence of AIDS antibodies in the blood.

The Western Blot also checks for antibodies to the AIDS virus. It is a more specific test—if it's positive, that means

QUESTIONS TO ASK

- What does a positive result mean?

- What does a negative result mean?

- Who will be notified of my test results?

- What record will be made of my test results, and who will have access to those records?

- Will my parents be notified?

- How will I be told about the test results—in person or on the phone?

- Will counseling be provided when I'm told my test results?

you have been exposed to the AIDS virus and are infected. The chance of an error with the Western Blot test is slim.

You can have your blood drawn for the ELISA test at nearly any doctor's office; it takes just a few minutes. But the blood sample must be sent to a lab for analysis, and you may have to wait several days to several weeks to get the results.

If you decide to get tested, you may want to do so at a center specifically set up to test people anonymously. Many cities have such places. By calling an AIDS hotline in your area or by calling the local public health department, you can find out where you can be tested, free of charge, without your parents' permission if you absolutely feel you can't tell them. (Some states require parental permission before providing the test for a minor.)

When you call to make an appointment, you are given a number and do not have to give anyone your name. When you actually get the test, your assigned number is attached to the tube containing the blood test. The test results cannot be traced back to you. They are anonymous.

Anonymous testing shouldn't be confused with confidential testing. The term "confidential" means that your doctor and others in your doctor's office know your test results, and that the information becomes part of your private medical record.

Be aware that insurance companies have a legal right to examine those records to determine whether they will sell you an insurance policy. Many insurance companies won't sell insurance to a person infected with HIV.

If you decide to be tested, first talk with the nurse, doctor, or counselor at the test center or doctor's office about what the test means and what it can and cannot tell you; for example, the test will not tell you whether you have AIDS, but only whether you have been exposed to the virus that causes AIDS. Counseling is routinely offered at testing sites. Be sure there is someone to talk to about AIDS if you are tested in a doctor's office.

Some people believe the best way to slow the spread of AIDS is to require that everyone be tested. Those who test positive would be able to take steps to stop spreading the virus, right?

It's not that simple.

To identify the estimated 1.5 million people thought to be infected with the AIDS virus in the United States, every citizen would have to be tested. Because it can take several months to develop antibodies to the AIDS virus—and more people are becoming infected every day—the government would have to test continuously. This would cost hundreds of millions of dollars.

Alexei: *"I think the worst thing about having AIDS would be that people would ostracize me because I have the virus. It would really destroy me if people shut me out of their lives because I had a disease."*

Tanya: *"You may think that you can't get AIDS and nothing bad can happen to you. You are wrong. No one is that superior. You should be afraid of getting AIDS and learn enough about it to prevent it."*

And what would we do with this information? Many infected people lead productive lives. Some are parents whose children depend on them. Others are teachers running classrooms or doctors caring for patients. And not every infected person develops AIDS. We couldn't possibly isolate or quarantine all these people—a solution that is both impractical and inhumane.

Some government agencies do have mandatory testing policies. For example, before enrollment in the Job Corps, the Peace Corps, or the military, applicants are required to take a blood test. The U.S. Immigration and Naturalization Service regulates immigration and the entry of non-U.S. citizens to the United States. The agency has strict rules that apply to people infected with the AIDS virus. And anyone immigrating to the United States is required to take a blood test. An infected person wishing to visit the United States can receive a waiver which allows him to travel here for 30 days.

Many people advocate that our time and money would be better spent on prevention and education. The best way to slow the spread of AIDS is to make sure people have the facts and protect themselves from the AIDS virus. This will help stop the spread of AIDS.

"SOME DAYS I FEEL LIKE I'M 18 GOING ON 60."

David has a dancer's body, broad shoulders and long, muscular legs. He says he was born to be a ballet dancer. An inscription in his baby book suggests he may be right. When he was a year and a half old, his mother wrote, "David loves to dance."

David, 18
Infected with
the AIDS virus

David danced through his childhood. In high school, he landed the leading role of a dancing sailor in the school play. All the attention helped bolster his self-image—and it helped his dancing career, too. Casting directors at a professional theater in a nearby town recognized his talent and gave him small parts in *Romeo and Juliet* and *Cinderella*.

"It was exciting to be around professional artists. And I liked that because I got to skip three weeks of school every time I was in a play."

The experience was invaluable. David learned a lot from the others in the theater. During his senior year in high school, he studied ballet at the prestigious North Carolina School of the Arts.

David danced four hours a day, five days a week. It paid off. He was offered a chance to study with the Hungarian International State Ballet. As he packed for Budapest, David became exhausted. Within a few days he was too weak to walk. As a gay man who had lost friends to AIDS, David was well informed. He knew he might have the disease. He cancelled his trip, and soon tests confirmed his fears.

"I started dealing with it in a very systematic, mechanical way. When I found out, I called up my mother and told her the test was positive and that I was going out to dinner. I didn't cry about it for at least six months."

Pushing AIDS to the back of his mind didn't mean David was able to forget about his illness. When you have AIDS, the reminders are there every day.

"Some days I wake up and feel like I am 18 going on 60. I wake up in the middle of the night and have a fever of 104°, which is scary. AIDS ages your body incredibly. Some mornings I wake up and I have no energy. It's just a matter of going back to bed and waking up the next day and hoping I feel stronger."

When he has good days, David makes the most of them. He accepted a job with the National AIDS Network, a group dedicated to educating people about AIDS and helping those who are infected. David travels across the country, warning young people about AIDS.

"You have to protect yourself. If you are having sex, make sure you have safer sex. And if you don't want to have sex, that's your right. It's nobody's business but yours."

Being busy doesn't protect David from loneliness. That is a big part of having AIDS.

"At times I feel like there is no one I can talk to. We all think about death at certain times, but I swear I never thought I'd have to think about it right after my 18th birthday. Being a teenager is hellish anyway. Drop AIDS into the picture and it becomes all the more confusing."

Barbara: *I think it's important to remember that it's* your *body and you* have to live with the decisions you make. So think hard about it before you act.

Chapter Eleven
DISCRIMINATION

I magine what it would be like if no one at school would talk to you. What if no one would sit near you in class or use the locker next to yours? What if people avoided you in the hallway? How would you feel if people were afraid to touch or hug you, or called you names? If you were infected with the AIDS virus, this might be the way you would be treated.

Many men, women, and children infected with the AIDS virus are given love and support by their families and friends. But thousands more become ostracized as a result of their disease. They are rejected by friends, family, and co-workers. As you read about Gil, try to imagine yourself in his shoes.

"PEOPLE WERE EVEN AFRAID OF MY MOTHER."

Gil, 23
Has AIDS

G il grew up in a small town in Texas. With 12 brothers and sisters, he learned how to get along with others.

Everyone in his family was expected to help out. By the time Gil was 11, he was earning money, working with his mother at a local fast-food restaurant. His $10 a week salary paid school bus fare for all the children.

"I had to help out. I didn't mind. The money my mother earned went for the bills she had to pay, things like food and clothing. We were never hungry. We had what we needed but there were 13 kids. There were a lot of expenses."

Gil was forced to grow up quickly. In a sense, he says, he never had a childhood. But taking on responsibilities as a youngster helped Gil prepare for challenges he would face as an adult.

When he graduated from high school, Gil was determined to become a chef. He enjoyed feeding people good food. He wanted to show his family that his hobby could earn him a living.

But Gil's best friend convinced him to do something else. Together, they signed up for nursing school. A year and a half later, having earned his nursing license, Gil applied for a job in a hospital. As a condition of his employment, he had to get a physical exam. Among the tests the doctors performed was one checking for presence of the AIDS virus. The test came back positive. It showed that Gil had been exposed to the AIDS virus. Gil knew he

Tanya: *"To discriminate against someone is inhumane."*

had been exposed through sex.

That was in 1985. Since then, Gil has experienced many HIV-related illnesses. But as he looks back, he says the emotional pain he has suffered because of discrimination has been far worse than any physical pain caused by his infection.

Even though the hospital knew Gil was infected with the AIDS virus, he was hired as a nurse. He took care of people with a wide range of diseases—"everything from cancer to AIDS." He liked the job. But after a few months, Gil became ill with AIDS-related pneumonia. He ended up a patient on his own ward, being cared for by his co-workers, who had not known Gil was infected with the AIDS virus. One particular nurse assigned to his case had been a special friend. They had gone out for drinks after work, talked, laughed, and enjoyed each other's company. Gil remembers the shock on her face the first time she walked into his hospital room.

Gil's friend refused to care for him. She never spoke to him again. Gil was crushed. He couldn't believe people trained in health care could be so ignorant. After a month in the hospital, Gil felt strong enough to return to work. But his boss told him the hospital no longer needed him and Gil was fired. Gil knew if he tried to be a nurse somewhere else, he would face the same scrutiny. But bills were coming in and rent was due, so Gil went to work in a restaurant.

"I told one friend at the restaurant that I was HIV-positive. It got back to the manager and I was fired from that job. They were afraid I would cut myself and bleed on the chicken."

Broke and depressed, he scrounged up enough money to buy a bus ticket home to his family. He knew they would take care of him. In Gil's small hometown, there were no secrets. Soon, neighbors found out Gil was sick with AIDS and they were afraid.

"My first encounter with people's fear was when I tried to get a suit cleaned. They refused to clean it because they thought if I had AIDS, my suit had AIDS. Then I went to a restaurant and they refused to serve me. People were even afraid of my mother. She had worked at the same restaurant for 19 years and people there started hassling her. They thought if her son had AIDS, she had AIDS."

Gil realized his neighbors were acting out of ignorance. He didn't hate them. But coping with it was exhausting, and the stress wore him down. He developed pneumonia again and had to be hospitalized. His hometown hospital turned him away. The doctors and nurses there had

PJ: *"If I got AIDS, I would be most worried about the isolation, about my friends not talking to me and not wanting to be with me because I had AIDS."*

never taken care of someone with AIDS, and they were afraid they might get infected. Without medical care, Gil knew he would die. His sister wrapped him up in blankets and drove him to another hospital 100 miles away where the staff reacted the same way and Gil was refused treatment a second time. Finally, a government-run hospital agreed to care for Gil.

Soon after Gil returned home from that hospital stay, he was attacked by someone who threw a rock at his head and knocked

"The pain my friends and I have felt due to the loss of those we love is overwhelming. Because of ignorance about how AIDS is transmitted, many people with AIDS have been abandoned by their friends. They have been deserted by their families. Some have lost their jobs and places to live. People with AIDS need your understanding, support, and compassion." —Brooke Shields, *Actress/model*

him unconscious. That was the final straw. Gil packed his bags and left home. But he didn't leave defeated.

"I have survived all this because I am a very strong person. I am fighting to keep alive. And I am winning. I have already come close to death so many times that I am not scared of that. I am not afraid of dying of AIDS. I am afraid someone will kill me before I die of AIDS."

Barbara: *"Prejudice against a person with AIDS is like racism and sexism. It's no different."*

Despite all the adversity in his life, more than four years after being diagnosed with AIDS Gil says he is happy. He has lots of friends and travels around the city of Tucson, where he lives, to teach student nurses about AIDS. And he is working once again as a nurse in a hospital where his boss knows he has AIDS. Gil makes sure his patients with AIDS get special love and attention. He considers life a gift that can be taken away any moment, and he is proving that it is possible to live a rich and meaningful life with AIDS.

"There is nothing to be afraid of. In time you will know a friend who has AIDS. The best thing to do is to take care of them. Give them support, listen to them, be by their side. I cry, and I need a shoulder to cry on. I laugh, and I need someone to laugh with. I hurt and I need someone to share my pain."

At the time Gil was fired, he was unaware that there are state and federal laws to protect people infected with the AIDS virus. In some states, it is illegal to fire or demote people because they are infected. And, in many states, it is illegal to test people for infection with the AIDS

"I REALIZED HOW MUCH I MUST HAVE HURT HIM."

"The first person I knew who had AIDS was an actor I worked with on an off-Broadway play called *Torch Song Trilogy*. I was very, very good friends with him. We used to really enjoy each other's company a lot. I'd roughhouse with him, you know, and I really loved him. Then he got sick with AIDS. It was early on, and nobody knew much about AIDS. I didn't know much about the ways you could get it. I heard that he was sick and then one day I ran into him in a restaurant. He told me he wanted to have lunch with me and talk. I was a little bit afraid to have lunch with him, so I called my doctor. The doctor told me, 'Well, you can have lunch with him, but don't drink out of his glass, don't take a bite of his food.' It scared me virus as a condition of employment. Gil didn't realize that it is illegal for a hospital to refuse care to people because they have AIDS—or for dry cleaners or other businesses to refuse to serve people with AIDS. If Gil had known that, he says he

enough that I never had lunch with my friend. I certainly wouldn't behave that way now, but that's what I did.

"About six months after my friend died, I was in an airport and there were some of those crazy people who walk around airports saying we should have more nuclear weapons. I overheard one say to another that they should drop a bomb on West Hollywood—that would clear up that AIDS problem. I looked at him and I was so angry that I couldn't say anything. I was just incredibly furious. As I left the airport and walked to my car, I thought of my friend who had died. I got into my car and just cried. I felt very badly that I hadn't gone to see him. It wasn't until then that I realized how much I must have hurt him. What those guys said showed the incredible discrimination against people with AIDS. Anyone suffering with AIDS should be treated with respect. People have to realize that it could just as easily be them who is sick. Learn as much as you can about AIDS. Talk about it. Tell each other about it. Don't separate yourself from people with AIDS. We all have to band together to help fight this disease. Everybody has to help."

—Matthew Broderick, *Actor*

would have taken legal action.

Congress and many states have passed laws protecting people from all types of discrimination. We most often hear about laws prohibiting discrimination against people because of their race, religion, or sex. These anti-discrimination laws also often protect people who are disabled or are perceived to be disabled.

People infected with the AIDS virus are considered disabled under federal and most state laws. These laws are designed to protect people like Gil.

These same laws also protect people like Gil's mother—who has suffered discrimination because people feared they could contract AIDS from her.

"Life is full of uncertainty. Being spontaneous and taking risks is an important part of life. But now, with AIDS in our midst, being adventurous with sex is dangerous. Be careful. Protect yourselves. AIDS kills."

—Cher, *Actress and singer*

If you want to find out what the laws are where you live, contact your local AIDS organization (see the list in the back of this book) or your state attorney general's office.

A WRITER LEARNS FROM "THE GUY WHO HAS AIDS"

Often people's attitudes change when they meet someone who has AIDS. Jessica Hitchcock, a high-school student in Yellow Springs, Ohio, wrote a story about meeting a man with AIDS. The article was printed on the front page of her hometown newspaper. In the following paragraphs, she describes what it was like to meet 18-year-old David.

"David. I will probably never see him again. But I will certainly never forget him. I went to an optional assembly to see 'the guy who has AIDS' and came away thinking of him simply as David. He was honest, self-confident, and friendly, the kind of person I would be proud to call a friend. As David talked with us about AIDS, I struggled to take the notes I needed for my newspaper article. My stomach was knotted, my vision blurred, I could barely take my eyes from his face. As he began to speak about his life at present, about how he was coping, his smile beamed determination and his laughter spread hope throughout the room. This is not the smile of a dying man, I thought. These are words that reveal promise, ambition. He is too young to be content. Only 18, he is too young to die.

"I wrote my article for the *Yellow Springs News* the day after I met David. My notes were scarce, consisting mostly of quotes I had scribbled without even looking at my notebook. I discovered, however, that his words had such an impact, I was able to write mostly from memory, from my heart. 'Go out and tell others what I have told you,' David said, 'That is what you can do for me.' David put a hopeful human face on a frightening fatal disease. 'Mortality,' David said. 'It's a difficult concept for someone to deal with, but it is especially difficult to come to terms with death when you are so young. Most of us are still starting to cope with life.'

"Perhaps being forced to realize his own mortality has enabled David to enjoy life as fully as he can. The people who have AIDS are not victims. It is the person who is misinformed, frightened, and angry who becomes the victim. It is the person who turns his or her back on David and others with AIDS who is impaired, for that person is missing the strength, courage, and love that David and the others who have come to terms with their disease have to share."

PEOPLE WITH AIDS NEED COMPASSION

Jeff, 31
Died from AIDS

On a warm, sunny day Jeff could be spotted speeding around Boston in his red convertible Saab. He made enough money as an investment banker to live in style. Jeff played as hard as he worked. He was an all-star shortstop in a softball league and would challenge anyone to a rigorous game of racquetball. Nearly every day Jeff ran, swam, or lifted weights. He was in spectacular physical condition.

A couple of years ago, Jeff left his job with the investment firm to travel around Massachusetts telling students his story. He thought they could learn a lot from a man who was living with AIDS. When he talked, teenagers paid attention.

He would start his story with some background.

"Before I tell you what life is like when you have AIDS, I'd like to tell you what it was like for me before I got AIDS. My educational background proves smart people can get AIDS, too. I went to Stanford University and graduated with a grade point average of 3.97. I went to Wharton Business School at the University of Pennsylvania, graduated with distinction in finance, and went to work as an investment banker in Boston. I had a com-

"Discriminating against someone who is suffering from AIDS is both unfair and closed-minded. Teenagers should try to gain a better understanding of the disease and should be more accepting of people who have become afflicted with AIDS. They should realize that without proper knowledge and protection, they too could become infected."

—Bo Jackson, *Baseball player*

fortable life with a nice 6-figure income."

While Jeff was with the investment firm, his co-workers didn't realize he was gay. Neither did his family. But when his lover of three years died from AIDS, Jeff knew it was time to tell them. How could he mourn the loss of someone he loved so much without telling those closest to him what had happened? It took courage, but Jeff revealed the whole story. No one rejected him. In fact, they responded with love and acceptance. Eight months later, Jeff was diagnosed with AIDS. Young people, hearing his story, can understand why people with AIDS need compassion. And he makes sure they understand that they, too, may be at risk for AIDS, even if they think they know the person with whom they are having sex.

"I've also slept with women in my life. Rhonda used a diaphragm and Patty used birth control pills. Neither do any good to protect against the AIDS virus. And I don't know how long I might have been infected before I was diagnosed. Patty and Rhonda are pretty worried right now, as you can imagine, wondering if I was infected when I was with them. Certainly I would feel terrible if I was."

Thousands of young people in Massachusetts were able to meet Jeff before he died. His family and friends take comfort in the fact that Jeff believed in a God that didn't turn His back on him because he was homosexual. As he told an auditorium full of high-school students, "Jesus healed the lepers of his day, and I guess I'm con-

HOW WOULD YOU FEEL?

The following exercise might help you get a sense of how it would feel to lose everything because of an illness.

Ask a friend, a brother or sister, or your parents to try this exercise with you. Maybe you can convince a teacher to include the exercise in a discussion about AIDS.

It's important that you keep your responses to yourself. Give each response plenty of thought and pay attention to the way you feel as you go through each step.

On a piece of paper write down:

1. a personal item that you value dearly

2. a personal or physical characteristic that makes you feel proud

3. your favorite physical activity

4. an important goal in your life for which you strive

5. a secret you have told only a few people, or no one at all

tent feeling that there is a special place in heaven for those people whom society doesn't have much use for."

6. a friend or loved one whose support has always meant a lot to you

Think about how important the items on this list are to you. Now imagine how you would feel if:

1. you lost the personal item you valued because you lost all your money

2. you had an accident and lost the physical attribute that made you feel proud

3. you were unable to do your favorite physical activity because of an accident

4. you were unable to achieve your goal because of the loss of money, the loss of your physical attribute, or your inability to perform a favorite physical activity

5. everyone you knew found out about your special secret

6. you lost your friend or loved one because of the changes named above

—From AIDS AND THE IV DRUG USER, published by the National Institute on Drug Abuse

Chapter Twelve

WHAT YOU CAN DO

Without an effective treatment or cure, education is the best defense we have against AIDS. There are a lot of creative ways to get the word out. Across the country young people are helping their friends, their brothers and sisters, and even their parents understand the facts about AIDS. You can help, too!

Iroquois Cowboys
Stone Mountain, Ga.
Keith Crutchfield,
Michael Wilson,
Andrew Wilson,
Bruce Parker

A POP GROUP GETS INVOLVED

The members of the Iroquois Cowboys describe their music as progressive, original pop. In the winter of 1989, they turned their passion for music into a fundraiser for AIDS. The event was called

Youth AID. Band member Keith Crutchfield got permission from his principal to use the high-school auditorium for a night. Four other local rock bands joined the Cowboys onstage and raised $600 for an Atlanta AIDS organization.

"In between sets," says Keith Crutchfield, "while each band was setting up, someone from AIDS-Atlanta would come up and talk into the microphone about how you can and cannot get AIDS. It was elementary, down-to-earth stuff. It was a good way to get something across to young people without preaching."

Keith says schools need to provide more AIDS education because AIDS is so prevalent in society. He's doing his part to help get out the warnings about the disease.

A HOTLINE FOR TEENAGERS

When Cara Morris first heard about AIDS, she was frightened. She realized a lot of her friends were putting themselves at risk for AIDS by having unprotected sex. Her friends, like

Cara Morris, 18
Started AIDS
hotline in Kansas
City, Missouri

a lot of other teenagers, thought the disease could affect only gay men and drug addicts.

"It was spreading to other populations and that was something people needed to find out about. At that time nothing in Kansas City, where I live, was targeted to teenagers."

So Cara and some other concerned teenagers went to work to change that. They formed TEENS TAP, or *Teens Teaching AIDS Prevention*. At monthly meetings, they plotted ways to spread warnings about AIDS. Their first move was to write a brochure describing how people can and can't get infected. Then they set up an AIDS hotline run for teenagers by teenagers.

"A lot of the time kids won't go to their parents to talk about safer sex or other questions about AIDS, and maybe they are embarrassed to go to their teachers. We figured if they had someone they could talk to on the phone, that would be the best way."

A $4,000 donation by two local doctors helped TEENS TAP install telephone lines. Office space was provided by a Kansas City AIDS service organization, The Good Samaritan. The phone number was advertised on national television, in newspapers, and in magazines. The telephones started ringing off the hook. Kids were calling from across the country.

"We get 300 to 400 calls a month. The most common calls are questions about how the virus is transmitted, how to identify symptoms, and how to protect themselves if they are going to have sex."

TEENS TAP was funded by a major grant from the prestigious Robert Woods Johnson Foundation. Cara says some days she can't believe that her organization has accomplished so much in so little time.

"You don't necessarily have to get involved in an AIDS organization. But if you can educate yourself and one of your friends, you will be doing quite a bit.

ART FOR AIDS AWARENESS

AIDS education poster designed by Robby Talamas, 18, of Sarasota, Florida

Walk into any school in Florida and chances are you will see this poster pinned to a bulletin board or taped to a wall. This creation of an 18-year-old high-school senior in Florida has come to represent the dangers of unprotected sex.

It won Robby Talamas first place in a poster contest sponsored by his high school to help raise AIDS awareness.

"I have posters hanging in my room and one of them is a joker. That's how I came up with the idea. I hope it sends a message to young people that you should be careful by not fooling around. When people my

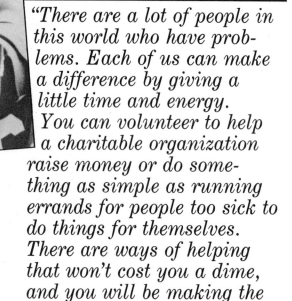

"There are a lot of people in this world who have problems. Each of us can make a difference by giving a little time and energy. You can volunteer to help a charitable organization raise money or do something as simple as running errands for people too sick to do things for themselves. There are ways of helping that won't cost you a dime, and you will be making the world a better place. It's a great feeling! Try it!"

—Joe Montana, *Professional football player*

age think about the word AIDS, I want them to think of my poster and realize AIDS is serious."

With his winning poster distributed all over the state, Robby was interviewed by newspapers and magazines. His friends are impressed. But for Robby, the biggest payback is knowing he has helped educate people about AIDS.

"By young people getting involved, I hope AIDS will never come to be a major problem for us. If we are aware about it now, we'll be better off in the future."

ONE SMALL WAY TO MAKE A DIFFERENCE

Robert Benjamin, 13
Newton,
Massachusetts
Donated money
to AIDS research

When Robert Benjamin turned 13, he celebrated an important day in his life, his bar mitzvah. His bar mitzvah marked his entrance into adulthood, according to Jewish custom, and Robert's parents threw him a party. Friends and relatives gave him gifts and money. Robert wanted to contribute some of that money to an important cause—sharing is a tradition in the Benjamin family.

"I thought since AIDS is one of the major things in the news today, and there are a lot of people who are suffering from it, it would be a nice thing to give money to AIDS research. I felt happy that I could help other people."

Robert included his friends in the gesture. As each guest arrived at the party, they were handed a scroll of paper tied with a blue ribbon. Inside, it said a donation had been given in their name to AIDS research. Robert says now, when they hear about AIDS, his friends will know that in their small way they have made a difference.

KIDS TEACHING KIDS

Chrissie Levinson,
17, Los Angeles,
California
Organized AIDS
seminar

Chrissie didn't think she would ever know anyone with AIDS. But after two of her friends died from the disease, she decided it was time to get involved with the issue.

After meeting a woman from a local AIDS service organization, Chrissie volunteered with a group called Adolescent Life. The group's purpose is to warn teenagers about AIDS.

"We have a group of peer counselors who meet at my house once a week, and we go over new facts about AIDS and write letters to people—like important people in Congress."

These student volunteers go into schools to educate other students about AIDS. They discuss everything from how the AIDS virus is transmitted to how to use a condom. And, Chrissie says, they laugh a lot. Kids teaching kids can have a good time while providing lifesaving information.

Chrissie feels most proud of organizing an AIDS awareness program for her classmates and their parents.

"In all, 300 showed up. In one room the kids went to a play about someone who got AIDS through a blood transfusion, while in another room the parents were talking to a psychologist. Then they swapped rooms so the kids were talking to the psychologist. The things that came up in that conversation were so great—I never thought the other kids would open up like that. It was really, really neat."

For days after the assembly, Chrissie was showered with compliments.

"I had kids come up to me and say they wanted another evening that was just for them. The headmaster of my school said it was a success and he wanted to do another one. It made me feel really good."

Because Chrissie took the initiative, kids in her school got a chance to talk about fears and thoughts in a different forum. Her efforts may have helped save a life.

"I decided when I was very young that I wanted to be an actor. Luckily, my parents supported my dream. When I first arrived in Hollywood, a casting agent told me I had no place in this business. I didn't buy that. Deep down inside, I believed in myself. So I surrounded myself with people who believed anything was possible —and here I am today! Listen, there will always be people trying to drag you down. Allow yourself to dream. Keep up your confidence and never, ever give up! And don't waste a minute on people who are negative."

—Danny DeVito, *Actor*

A COLLEGE FUNDRAISER

Leslie Chertok, 23
Boulder, Colorado
Held dance-a-thon
for AIDS

Once a year, students at Leslie Chertok's college hold a dance-a-thon for charity. Last year, students at New College in Sarasota, Florida, voted to donate the money to an AIDS organization. Sixteen students signed up sponsors and danced away for 24 hours. Leslie says the event was exhausting but fun. When the music stopped and the dancers went home to sleep, Sarasota AIDS Support had an additional $3,000 in the bank.

"The volunteers danced 50 minutes of every hour and then took 10 minutes off for catnaps and massages. But lots of other students got involved, too. It was like a giant party. All kinds of food had been donated and kids were serving pizza, fried chicken, bagels, and ice cream. The director of housing came and cooked Swedish crepes for breakfast. Other people were mixing tapes and we even had a massage therapist there."

For the last few hours of the dance-a-thon, a live band kept the dancers energized. Leslie recalls that the highlight of the evening was a visit from a man with AIDS.

"Right before the grand finale when

everyone was numb and giddy, a gentleman with AIDS, on the board of directors of S.A.S., came to talk to us. He said, 'I can see you are so fatigued. Most people don't realize that feeling. But if you talk to people who have AIDS, most days of their lives are spent feeling that fatigued.' I was exhausted at the time, and I thought that must be really tough to wake up that exhausted after sleeping nine hours. It really brought it home for me."

Leslie believes that the burden of AIDS will fall on the shoulders of people of her generation. So she suggests they get involved in doing their part to fight the epidemic.

"Even if you are not going to be super sexually active or use drugs, it is the youth who are going to be suffering. It's their friends who will be dying from it, and they will be paying for it financially."

Darlene Goding, 18
Topsfield, Ma.
Designed T-shirt
logo

HEARTS LINKED FOR AIDS

Darlene Goding doesn't understand why some people with AIDS are treated so poorly. She feels bad when she reads about an infected child kept out of school, or a family harassed by neighbors because a family member has AIDS.

During a three-day AIDS seminar in her school, she met the director of a local AIDS organization, called Strongest Link. He was recruiting people to participate in a local AIDS walk-a-thon. Darlene signed up and agreed to design T-shirts to be sold at the walk.

"I thought people with AIDS in this society aren't getting the love and attention they should be getting, so I used hearts linking like a chain would link. It symbolizes people caring for one another. We printed 120 T-shirts and they all sold. We profited over $720 for the care of people with AIDS."

Darlene is proud of her contribution. When she walks down the street in her hometown, she passes people who have bought her T-shirts.

"I get really happy that there are people out there who want to help, like my friends who will support a cause like AIDS and not really care what other people think. When I see people wearing one of my T-shirts, I know these are people that want the best for people with AIDS."

Young Nation
Todd, Bobby,
Michael, Tshombe,
Dramayne
Boston,
Massachusetts

MUSIC WITH A MESSAGE

I'm gonna say this rhyme
Just to let you all know that
This disease is just
*   So damn thoughtless . . .*
Use a condom, if you're
having sex, Or, Homeboy, don't have sex.

These are lyrics by Young Nation, a Boston rap group. At a recent fund-raiser for AIDS at a nightclub in Boston, Young Nation brought down the house with their rap music. These guys believe their "music with a message" teaches young people about the dangers of AIDS faster and better than any 30-second television announcement.

These five talented guys could write and rap about anything. They chose AIDS because they know it's a disease with no cure. And they are serious about doing their part to save lives.

Todd: "It's fun making music, and I love it, but if someone can learn from our music then that makes it a whole lot better."

Tshombe: "I hope kids listen to what we are saying and remember the next time they're about to do something dumb, to think about where they might end up."

Bobby: "This is our world. We have to make it better. We can't wait for a miracle to happen. We have to make it happen. People need to understand more about AIDS."

Dramayne: "They say we are the future. If we're not smart about AIDS there will be no future."

Michael: "I have a cousin who has AIDS. I hope our rap gets out to everyone so that nobody has to go through what he is going through."

"EVERYONE NEEDS EDUCATION"

Kareem Brown was deeply moved when he read about a boy being kept out of school because he had AIDS. You see, Kareem realized the same thing could have happened to him. At the age of three, Kareem had a blood transfusion during heart surgery. Fortunately, the blood he got was not infected with the AIDS virus. He was so touched by the story, he decided to look into the issue and report on it for his school's social science fair.

Kareem Brown, 12
Decatur, Georgia
Researched AIDS
for social science
fair

"I wrote to various principals who had children with AIDS in their school. Then I wrote to organizations across the country that dealt with AIDS. I asked them to give me their opinion about whether children with AIDS should attend public school. I learned that communities that didn't know much about AIDS were treating the children poorly. But the communities that knew the facts about AIDS were treating their children like anyone else."

His research taught Kareem the value of AIDS education. As the epidemic spreads, Kareem warns, other children could be denied an opportunity to go to school with their friends. He says school boards and principals should deal with the issue now, before a crisis hits.

"Everyone needs education. Sooner or later, someone is going to get AIDS in your community and you need to be ready for it—with the right information."

THE NAMES PROJECT

Perhaps you have heard of the AIDS memorial quilt, which is made up of thousands of 3' by 6' panels decorated with ribbons, sequins, jewelry, and many other materials. Each panel represents someone who has died from AIDS.

The AIDS quilt,
Washington, D.C.

The first panel was sewn in San Francisco by Cleve Jones, who has lost many friends to AIDS. Now more than 11,000 panels from across the United States make up this memorial.

In the fall of 1989, the entire quilt was displayed in Washington, D.C., across the street from the White House. It covered a space larger than eight football fields. Because the quilt has grown so large it will never be seen again in one piece. Smaller displays will continue to tour, and panels will be added as more lives are lost to AIDS.

You can find out more about this memorial, and how to contribute to it, by calling or writing to:

Names Project
2362 Market Street
San Francisco, CA 94114
415-863-5511

INFORMATION

NATIONAL AIDS HOTLINE
1-800-342-AIDS

STATE AIDS HOTLINES

ALABAMA
1-800-228-0469

ALASKA
1-800-478-AIDS

ARIZONA
1-800-342-AIDS

ARKANSAS
1-800-445-7720

CALIFORNIA
NORTHERN
1-800-367-AIDS
SOUTHERN
1-800-922-AIDS

COLORADO
1-800-252-AIDS

CONNECTICUT
1-800-874-2572 or
1-800-342-AIDS

DELAWARE
1-800-422-0429

**DISTRICT OF
COLUMBIA**
1-800-332-AIDS

FLORIDA
1-800-FLA-AIDS

GEORGIA
1-800-551-2728

HAWAII
1-800-321-1555

IDAHO
1-800-833-AIDS

ILLINOIS
1-800-AID-AIDS

INDIANA
1-800-848-AIDS

IOWA
1-800-445-AIDS

KANSAS
1-800-232-0040

KENTUCKY
1-800-654-AIDS

LOUISIANA
1-800-99-AIDS-9

MAINE
1-800-851-AIDS

MARYLAND
1-800-638-6252

MASSACHUSETTS
1-800-235-2331

MICHIGAN
1-800-872-AIDS

MINNESOTA
1-800-248-AIDS

MISSISSIPPI
1-800-826-2961

MISSOURI
1-800-533-AIDS

MONTANA
1-800-233-6668

NEBRASKA
1-800-782-AIDS

NEVADA
1-800-842-AIDS

NEW HAMPSHIRE
1-800-752-AIDS

NEW JERSEY
1-800-624-2377

NEW MEXICO
1-800-545-AIDS

NEW YORK
1-800-342-AIDS

NORTH CAROLINA
1-800-342-AIDS

NORTH DAKOTA
1-800-472-2180

OHIO
1-800-342-AIDS

OKLAHOMA
1-800-522-9054

OREGON
1-800-777-AIDS

PENNSYLVANIA
1-800-692-7254

RHODE ISLAND
1-800-342-AIDS

SOUTH CAROLINA
1-800-322-AIDS

SOUTH DAKOTA
1-800-592-1861

TENNESSEE
1-800-525-AIDS

TEXAS
1-800-299-AIDS

UTAH
1-800-537-1046

VERMONT
1-800-882-AIDS

VIRGINIA
1-800-533-4148

WASHINGTON
1-800-272-AIDS

WEST VIRGINIA
1-800-642-8244

WISCONSIN
1-800-334-AIDS

WYOMING
1-800-327-3577

CANADIAN AIDS HOTLINES

AIDS CLEAR-ING HOUSE
1-613-725-3769

OTTAWA
1-613-568-AIDS

TORONTO
1-416-392-AIDS

ACKNOWLEDGMENTS

Risky Times is a reflection of the time, energy, expertise, and concern of many people including: Jack Armitage, Kevin Cranston, Dr. Robert Dale, Bruce Decker, Marc Fournier, Jim Frances, Dr. Murray Feingold, Kenneth Fishkin, Esq., Robert Greenwald, Esq., Dr. Jerome Groopman, Diane Handler, John Hogan, Larry Kessler, Richard Knox, Joyce Kulhawik, Sandy Lefebvre, Dick McKnight, Soledad O'Brien, Dr. Peter Page, Nancy Carlsson-Paige, Judi Paparelli, Carole Pastan, Anne Peacher, Sister Marie Puleo, Shoshana Rosenfeld, Betty Russell, Jack Thomas, and Jules Verdone.

Through her many photographs in this book, Loel Poor helps put a human face on AIDS. She generously supported me and this project.

Thank you Tanya, Ben, Alexei, PJ, Barbara, and Aaron for trusting me.

I am indebted to Peter Workman for saying yes to my proposal for Risky Times, to Workman Publishing editors Karen Watts and Elisabeth Scharlatt, whose insight and skill created a book from my manuscript, and to Jonathan Dolger, my agent, for bringing us together.

Thomas Goodgame, John Spinola, and

Stan Hopkins, of Westinghouse Broadcasting, enthusiastically supported my desire to write a book.

My husband, Kent Damon, and my stepsons, Kyle and Matthew Damon, bolstered me with their love, support, patience, and ideas.

PHOTOGRAPHY CREDITS

Author photo, p. 7: Loel Poor; *All photos of Alexei, Ben, Tanya, PJ, Barbara, and Aaron:* Loel Poor; *Ali Gertz, pp. 14, 47, 64:* Jim Frances; *Whitney Houston, p. 19:* Richard Avedon; *John, p. 21:* Jim Frances; *Whoopi Goldberg, p. 22:* Courtesy of Whoop, Inc.; *Darren, p. 31:* Kent Damon; *Bobby Brown, p. 32:* Todd Grey; *Carolyn, p. 34:* Jim Frances; *Carolyn and Roy, p. 37:* Jim Frances; *Barbara, p. 40:* Loel Poor; *Barbara and Alice, p. 43:* Loel Poor; *Susan Dey, p. 45:* Brigitte Jouxtel; *Steve Tyler, p. 52:* Dennis Keeley; *Alan Kramer, p. 54:* Betty Russell; *Larry Bird, p. 68:* Courtesy of the Boston Celtics; *Alison, pp. 69, 71, 74:* Loel Poor; *Robert, p. 76:* Loel Poor; *Larry Aaronson, p. 78:* Patrick Kennedy; *Eddie Murphy, p. 81:* Courtesy of the Terrie Williams Agency; *Jashine, p. 83:* Loel Poor; *Deborah, p. 85:* Loel Poor; *Dr. Lorraine Hale, p. 88;* Courtesy of Hale House; *Eddie, pp. 90–94:* Loel Poor; *Jack Armitage, p. 95:* Loel Poor; *Dr. Lewllys Barker, p. 101:* Courtesy of American Red Cross National Headquarters; Heather Kamens; David Kamens; *Gil, p. 118:* Joel Gray; *Brooke Shields, p. 122:* Patrick Demarchelier; *Matthew Broderick, p. 124:* Kerry Hayes; *Cher, p. 126:* Herb Ritts; *Jeff, p. 129:* Courtesy of Andy Barmeyer; *Bo Jackson, p. 130:* Courtesy of the Chicago White Sox; *The Iroquois Cowboys, p. 134:* Bob Crutchfield; *Cara Morris, p. 135:* Marvin Elmore; *Joe Montana, p. 138:* Courtesy of the San Francisco 49ers; *Robert Benjamin, p. 139:* Betty Russell; *Chrissie Levinson, p. 140;* Michael Lamont; *Danny DeVito, p. 142:* Courtesy of Stan Rosenfield Public Relations; *Darlene Goding, p. 144;* Loel Poor; *Young Nation, p. 146:* Pierre Vallete; *Kareem Brown, p. 147:* Ethel Brown; *The AIDS quilt, p. 149:* Nancy Bland.

Jeanne Blake is a medical reporter in Boston. Her coverage of the AIDS epidemic led Massachusetts Governor Michael Dukakis to present her with the Governor's Recognition Award for her "outstanding contributions to AIDS education in Massachusetts," and she was given the Massachusetts Public Health Association's Public Service Award for her "significant contributions of public service in behalf of public health." Blake has been honored by human rights organizations, teachers' groups and health care professionals for her work on AIDS and other health care issues. She lives in Boston with her husband and two teenage stepsons.

This book comes with a free guide to help parents be AIDS-smart, too. You can order an additional copy of *The Parents' Guide to Risky Times*, by Beth Winship, author of the popular syndicated column "Ask Beth." Write to:

Workman Publishing
Educational Sales Dept.
708 Broadway
New York, NY 10003

A packet of 10 is available for $2.00, for postage and handling. Write to us if you want more information.